He Lives

HEATHER GUTTSCHUSS

Pacific Press Publishing Association
Boise, Idaho
Oshawa, Ontario, Canada

Edited by Don Mansell
Cover calligraphy by James O'Halloran
Design by Tim Larson
Type set in 11/13 Century Schoolbook

The author assumes full responsibility for the accuracy of all facts cited in this book. To protect those concerned some names of people and places have been changed.

Library of Congress Card Catalog Number: 87-63359

ISBN–0-8163-0743-1

88 89 90 91 92 • 5 4 3 2 1

DEDICATED TO

All who generously shared
their time and experiences:
Eric Armer, F. A. Botomoni, the Cordrays, Carl Currie,
Bill Edsell, Alan Handysides, Nicodemus Kahari, Faye
Kitney, Ken Mittleider, R. R. Ndholvu, Rex Pearson, and
all who have experienced God's greatness.

Preface

"It doesn't seem as though God works many miracles these days," a friend recently remarked to me.

Immediately I countered with, "Haven't you heard about the church overrun with bees? Or about the Bible that wouldn't burn?"

From the blank look on my friend's face I knew that he had not heard. Yet how could he have missed these stories when we both live and work in Africa? That's when I began collecting the stories that you will find in this book. These are stories that have all recently happened or are happening today. They are stories of God's miracles in Malawi, Tanzania, Ethiopia, Uganda, Kenya, Zambia, Zimbabwe, and Botswana—countries that make up the Eastern Africa Division.

As God's greatness has been revealed over and over, I have been reminded of Jethro's statement when Moses recounted to him the way God had miraculously led the people out of Egypt. Jethro exclaimed, "Praise be to the Lord! Now I know that God is greater than all other gods."

As you read, may you also exclaim, "Praise the Lord! God is indeed greater!"

Contents

Chapter 1
God Is Greater

The silence of the night was shattered by Paul's scream. "Help! I'm choking!"

Paul's cries banished sleep from his groggy brain. "Help me! Help me!" he yelled. But no help came. "What kind of nightmare is this?" he wondered frantically. Then all of a sudden he realized that this was no dream. He could feel a man's fingers tightening around his neck. He awoke in a cold sweat.

Fighting for his life, Paul struggled to get out of bed, wrestling frantically with his unseen assailant. He pulled and shoved with all his might, trying to break the viselike stranglehold the man had around his neck.

"Get out of here!" Paul yelled, but his screams were stifled in his throat. His assailant, whom he could not see because of the darkness, continued to tighten his grip.

"He's going to kill me!" Paul thought wildly. "How did this man get into our house and why is he trying to kill *me?*"

Paul had always wanted to be a missionary to Africa. Ever since he was a small boy, he had wanted to serve his Lord—but not just anywhere—no, he wanted to serve Him in Africa. Africa fascinated him.

It titillated his imagination. So, when he and his wife, Judy, and their two boys, Jeff and Greg, arrived in Zimbabwe, it was a dream come true.

Paul threw himself with enthusiasm into his work as director of the union publishing department. Thirstily he drank in the new sights and sounds around him—donkey carts on city streets, women clad in bright-colored clothes carrying loads of wood precariously perched on top of their heads, small children with outstretched hands, eager for a hand-out, and the occasional call of a hyena at night. Everything seemed enveloped in a strange tropical aura, and Paul loved every bit of it!

One morning Paul met Pastor Zhou during worship at the mission office. He didn't realize it at the time, but Pastor Zhou was destined to change his life in more ways than he could have imagined just then.

It all began when Pastor Zhou said, "I once knew a witch doctor who accepted Jesus as his Saviour. Before he was baptized, he brought all the tools he used in his craft and gave them to me—his well-used drum, a set of divining bones, his black robe, and a feathery head-dress. 'I don't need these anymore,' he declared. 'From now on I'm going to work for God, not the devil.' To give up these objects was a real turnabout for this man who for years had used these objects to cast spells, heal dis-eases, and commune with evil spirits. But not only did he part with these objects, he demonstrated his decisive break with the forces of evil by being baptized in the river near his village."

Pastor Zhou's remarks sparked Paul's thought processes.

"I'd like to see those drums and bones the witch doc-tor used! Maybe I could even own some," he mused. "If I could show the people back in the homeland the paraphernalia a witch doctor uses in his work, I could help them better understand God's power to change lives."

Paul's thoughts tumbled on. "Just think how impressed people would be. I've got an idea! I'll ask Pastor Zhou to let me have them."

"May I have the converted witch-doctor's tools?" Paul asked.

"I'm sorry," said Pastor Zhou. "I have already promised them to someone else. But I'll tell you what I will do. I'll keep your request in mind, and next time a witch doctor is converted and gives up his gear, I'll give it to you."

Paul thanked Pastor Zhou and was about to leave when the pastor cautioned, "Before I give you a witch-doctor's tools, I think I should warn you that they are nothing to be trifled with. Even though a witch doctor has been converted and has given them up, they continue to be the tools of the devil.

"Let me explain," continued Pastor Zhou. "I recall one experience when we tried to dispose of a witch-doctor's special medicines. The sorcerer had been baptized and wanted to forget about his old, past life. He gave me a cow's horn filled with strong herbal medicines. We decided to burn it. A fire was burning by the ex–witch-doctor's hut, and we threw the horn into the flames; but it hadn't been there for more than a minute when, to everyone's surprise, it jumped out!"

Paul laughed. Pastor Zhou continued, "So, we threw the horn into the fire again, and it jumped right back out! We threw it in the third time with the same results. The horn simply would not stay in the fire! It would not burn!"

"So, what did you do?" asked Paul.

"We decided that if we couldn't burn the horn, we would drown it. We took it to the river and threw it in.

That did it. This time the horn didn't jump back out. It sank, and as it disappeared from sight, we heaved a sigh of relief." Pastor Zhou paused.

"Whether we realize it or not, Satan is alive and active. I have seen him at work. But I also know that God's power is stronger than Satan's and that a witch-doctor's discarded tools can be convincing evidence to people in your missionary homeland. It is tangible evidence that God does transform lives. So, next time a witch-doctor accepts Christ, I will remember your request."

Later, as Paul thought about Pastor Zhou's words of warning, he wasn't so sure he wanted to own a witch-doctor's tools. It almost seemed to him as if owning them was like stepping over on the devil's ground. He seriously considered telling Pastor Zhou he had changed his mind. But then, he thought about it some more, and finally decided that surely there'd be no harm in having a few artifacts to show the people back in the homeland. After all, he rationalized, he only wanted these articles to impress the people with God's power. And so, he dismissed any thought of telling Pastor Zhou he had changed his mind, and it wasn't long before he'd all but forgotten about his request and Pastor Zhou's promise.

Tucked away in the sun-parched mountains, not far from where Paul lived, a little village spread its grass-roofed huts across the rugged landscape. Sitting just outside his hut in the shade of its overhanging roof, Bonipa, a witch-doctor, lazily tossed a wad of chewing tobacco into his mouth. Leaning back against the mud-brick wall of his hut, he smiled contentedly.

"What a life," he gloated half aloud. "Look at all the cattle I own. Look at the goats, the chickens. I am a rich man. Everyone comes to me for healing, and I always have the power to help them. The spirits I talk to are good to me. I don't have a worry in the world."

Just then Bonipa's wife poked her head around the corner of the open door and asked, "Were you talking to me?"

"Oh no, not really. I was just thinking out loud and congratulating myself on how well-to-do we are. All the people come to me with their troubles, and I have answers. Everything is going so well." He smiled a satisfied smile.

Bonipa's wife busied herself sweeping the yard. After a few minutes of thoughtful silence she spoke.

"Have you noticed that recently more and more people are going to listen to the new preacher over the hill in the next village? His medicine must be powerful, for it draws the people back again and again."

The smile of satisfaction vanished from Bonipa's face. His mood suddenly changed, and his words became short and crisp. "Yes, I have noticed that what you say is true! But I don't believe his medicine is better than mine." Then, as if doubting his own words, he added, "What could he possibly have that I don't have?"

"I don't know," answered his wife. "But don't worry. Everyone for miles around here believes in your powers, so don't give it a thought. You will always be a wealthy man."

Bonipa's self-satisfied smile returned. But as time passed, he couldn't help but notice that, since the arrival of the new lay preacher, fewer and fewer clients came to consult him. Some of these people brought him chickens, others eggs, still others a goat or a cow. The decline in these gifts was sure evidence that Bonipa was earning less than he used to.

"What medicine does the new lay preacher have that I don't have?" Bonipa asked himself one day. "I wonder if he would sell me some of his magic potion."

Gradually the idea began to form in Bonipa's mind. "I'm going to have to see this preacher. I've simply got to find out what kind of special medicine he uses that is drawing so many of my clients away from me."

So, early one morning before daylight, Bonipa started out to visit the lay preacher. When he reached the village where the lay preacher lived, he asked the first group of people he met where the man lived. He also asked them about his medicine. "Yes, he has powerful medicine," the villagers chorused in agreement. "He teaches us wonderful things. Come with us, and we will show you where he lives."

When Bonipa met the lay preacher, he hurried through the customary African greetings and went directly to the purpose of his visit. "What kind of medicine do you have that draws so many people to you?" he asked his host with evident curiosity. "I have lived and worked with the people in my village for many years, but I have never known anything to attract them like your medicine does. What *is* your medicine?" he demanded.

The lay preacher smiled. "I feed the people."

"Feed the people?" A questioning look came over Bonipa's face. "What do you mean you 'feed the people'?"

"I feed the people the Word of God. That is my medicine. It is powerful and it heals."

"But I have power too," countered Bonipa. "I can heal all kinds of sicknesses. There aren't many diseases I can't heal. I have much power!" he boasted.

"You may heal physically," explained the lay preacher. "I heal spiritually, and that kind of healing changes people. It changes their minds, their bodies, and their hearts. The kind of healing you do doesn't change people's hearts."

"What do you mean, your kind of healing 'changes people's hearts'? " Bonipa puzzled.

"My medicine heals people on the inside," the layman continued to explain.

"So does mine," rejoined Bonipa.

Patiently the lay preacher continued to explain. "You may heal the tissues of the body, but you do not heal the person's life. The medicine I give makes bad people good. It makes people who are mean kind and loving.

"You are a witch doctor, are you not?" Bonipa nodded. "As a witch doctor, you practice witchcraft. When someone comes and asks you to put a curse on an enemy, you do as you are asked. Sometimes the curse causes great harm. My treatment book, the Bible, says we should not hurt anybody. It says we should love our enemies just as much as we love ourselves. This means no curses, no evil practices, no harmful medicines."

Bonipa listened with wonder. He had never heard anyone talk like this before.

"Why don't you stay for the meeting today and eat some of the food I'm going to give the people," invited the lay preacher. "If you take the medicine from my Book, you will find new joy. We are having a meeting tonight. Why don't you come and take some of the food I'm going to give?" the lay preacher urged.

Although Bonipa was curious, he didn't attend the meeting that night. He decided to go home and think over what he had heard. Nor did he come to the meetings the next day nor for a whole week. But all this time he was thinking about what the lay preacher had told him.

By the time the second week rolled around, Bonipa's curiosity had gotten the better of him. One day he walked over to the lay preacher's village and listened to him speak—even though he sat under a tree some distance from the preacher. The third week Bonipa edged closer to the thatched area where the preacher stood. And by the fourth week Bonipa was attending every meeting and sitting right up front.

"I *like* your food," he told the lay preacher after one meeting. "But," and he paused before he continued, "I'm not ready to *eat* it. Not yet."

Before long the lay preacher began another series of meetings. Bonipa attended faithfully. This time, instead of just sitting quietly drinking in all that was said, he came armed with all sorts of questions. He especially wanted to know about what happens to dead people.

"How can the lay preacher say that the dead don't know anything, when I talk to them all the time?" he wondered within himself.

"What your book says can't be true!" Bonipa stoutly objected one evening. "I talk to the spirits of the dead all the time, and they answer me, so I know they're alive. They *do* know something. Your Bible isn't telling the truth!"

There was a stir among the people. Some murmured agreement with Bonipa. After all, hadn't they seen his little tin can with a mirror, on the bottom of which was attached a string. Hadn't they watched him pull the string taut, seen him ring his little silver-colored bell, and heard him summon the spirits? Why, they had heard him converse with the spirits through it. They had witnessed the results of the instructions he received from them. "No," they concluded, "the spirits of our ancestors are not dead!" Of this they were sure.

When the murmuring quieted down, the lay preacher continued, "You may think that when you speak with the spirits you are speaking to the spirits of the dead, but you are mistaken," he explained. "Instead, you are talking to the spirits of devils."

A sudden hush came over the people.

"The devil is very clever," he went on. "He can make himself look and speak just like your dead loved ones. He can give correct answers to your questions. But he does this to gain your confidence. Then, when he has your confidence, he mixes in lies in order to deceive you. On the other hand, the God of heaven only tells the truth."

The lay preacher now spoke directly to Bonipa. "God is telling the truth when He says that the dead do not know anything. Because the devil cannot be seen but can make himself seen when he wants to, he pretends to be the dead person. He is the one who has made you think you were talking to the dead."

Confident that most of his audience now agreed with him by the way they reacted, the lay preacher turned to the people and asked, "Do you agree?" Many heads nodded agreement.

"The dead are fast asleep," he continued. "They don't know anything about what goes on in the world. *They know nothing!*" The lay preacher emphasized this last sentence.

Bonipa swallowed hard. This was strange medicine. He'd need time to think about it before committing himself.

"Have I really been speaking to the spirits of devils instead of the dead as I've always thought?" he asked himself.

Bonipa continued to attend the meetings faithfully. As they came to a close, he announced, "I have decided to accept your food. I want to join your church." But a smile tugged at the corners of his mouth as he added,

"But I will also continue to be a witch doctor."

Patiently the lay preacher explained, "You cannot serve God and the devil. If you choose to serve God, you will have to get rid of the things you use in your witchcraft—your witch-doctor's clothes, the things you use to talk to the spirits. All these things you must give up."

"But I don't want to give them up," Bonipa stated firmly. "I need them. If I give up my medicine-filled kudu horn, how will I stop lightning from striking? How will I know what to do if I give up my herbal cup and can't speak to the spirits anymore? They tell me everything I want to know. I can't give them up. I *can't!*"

It was plain to all that an inner conflict was raging inside Bonipa as he turned and plodded his way home. He was determined to continue to be a witch doctor, but try as he might, he couldn't get the words of the lay preacher out of his head—"the dead do not know anything."

Weeks went by. Patients came to Bonipa's hut and patients left. But there were days when none came.

"You look tired," his wife said to him one day. "Is something troubling you, Bonipa? Is it that lay preacher?"

Bonipa looked up at his wife, but said nothing.

"Fewer and fewer patients are coming to you now," she observed. "Before, we used to get many cows and goats and chickens. Now we hardly get any. It is not like it was in the past. What has happened?"

Bonipa's wife waited for a reply. She sensed that her husband was wrestling with the things he had learned from the lay preacher. Ever since attending the meetings his days had been restless, his nights troubled. Things couldn't go on this way much longer.

His despondency troubled his wife.

When Bonipa finally spoke his voice was strained. Each word came slowly and with agonized effort. "No, it's not the same anymore," he admitted. "Now the spirits taunt me when I ring the bell to summon them. When I speak to them, they hesitate. It's as if they don't want to answer me anymore." He sighed, thought a moment, then added, "And yet, the spirits *do* answer me, and their medicines are what the people want."

He paused, then continued. "As you know, wife, for years the people have come to me for healing. Witchcraft is all I know. How can I give it up? If I give it up, what can I do for a living? I don't know any other work. What will happen to our family? And besides, what will the people say?"

He paused again before continuing. "If I give up witchcraft and follow a God I cannot hear or see, the people will accuse me of giving them medicine I do not believe in." He groaned. "Is it possible that my medicine has been all lies? Has the devil tricked me all these years? What have I done to deserve this?"

After a while Bonipa's wife spoke. "You are a good man, my husband. You have always done your work well. Everyone knows this is true. Do not fear; do not be anxious about our future."

Bonipa said nothing, but sat thinking.

Long before sunrise Bonipa got up out of bed. Without a word to anyone, not even his wife, he took his walking stick and began trudging his way toward the lay preacher's village. When he entered the settlement clearing he hesitated. "Is this really what I should do?" he asked himself. "Am I really making the right decision?" His resolve trembled in the balance, but only for a moment. "Yes, this is the right decision," he said resolutely to himself. "Of this I'm sure!"

When he arrived at the lay preacher's house, the lay preacher invited him in. After the customary African greetings, Bonipa told him the purpose of his visit.

"I've been watching you for many weeks," he told the lay preacher, "and I have been thinking." He paused, searching for the right words. "Your medicine is strong medicine. It is good medicine. I have decided to take your medicine. I want to join your church!"

"Praise God," rejoiced the lay preacher. "I have been praying for a long time that you would come to this decision. I have prayed that you would give your whole life to Jesus."

Now the lay preacher asked, "But what about all the things you use in your witch doctoring? Are you willing to give them up? What about the instructions from the spirits? Are you willing to stop talking to them?"

"I shall give them *all* up," Bonipa answered with a smile of determination. "I want to talk with your God— the God who is alive. I don't want to talk to the spirits anymore. I want to join your church right away."

The lay preacher smiled as he clasped Bonipa's hand. "You'll never be sorry you've made this decision," he assured him. "You have made a wise and wonderful choice. You have begun a new life."

But now a troubled look crossed Bonipa's face. "I agree with what you say, but I have a problem," he said. "I don't know how I will make a living. How shall I feed and clothe my family? Right now I am a rich man. I have many cows, goats, and chickens, but they will not last forever, and when they are gone, what shall I do for a living? I don't know any other kind of work, and I am too old to learn a new job. All I know is witchcraft."

It was clear to the lay preacher that Bonipa had been thinking seriously about the difficult decision he had made. He could see that Bonipa knew that his decision would require sacrifice, but he was glad that Bonipa was determined to follow through on his life-changing decision, cost what it may.

As the lay preacher looked across the large expanse of land that spread out before him, the thought suddenly struck him. "Why couldn't Bonipa take up farming?" Turning to the former witch-doctor, he said, "Go back to your village and be a farmer. You learned how to till the soil when you were a boy, didn't you?"

Bonipa nodded.

The lay preacher continued, "Well, be a farmer again. Put in more crops this year than you did last year, and I am sure God will bless. God promises to 'supply all your need according to his riches in glory by Christ Jesus,'" he quoted from the Bible. "And, as you live among your people," he continued, "live the new life in Jesus. Let the people in your village see that you no longer hurt people or place curses on them. Let them see that you are now a new man—God's man—filled with God's love and His spirit. Tell your wife about your decision and talk it over with your family. Ask them to join you in your decision. I will arrange for Pastor Citwala to study the Bible further with you."

Bonipa agreed to the suggestion, and soon Pastor Citwala began a series of Bible studies with him that lasted four months. As the studies progressed, the ex–witch doctor marveled at the way God solved the problems that had troubled him so much. As the studies neared their conclusion, he grew more and more convinced that the Bible speaks the truth. And the more he studied the more he wanted to be baptized.

"When can I be baptized?" he asked anxiously one day.

Camp-meeting time was nearing, and Pastor Citwala felt certain that Bonipa would be ready for the sacred rite by that time.

"A preacher is coming to our camp meeting," the pastor told Bonipa one day. "He will be here for a whole week. He will preach and pray and study the Bible with us. When he comes, we will ask him to baptize you."

"Who is this man?" Bonipa wanted to know.

"He is the field president in one of the neighboring countries. His name is Pastor Zhou. I know you will want to meet him."

Bonipa looked forward to his baptism with joyous anticipation. But as the eventful day approached, he began to wonder if Pastor Zhou would find him ready. Would he be able to answer all the questions? He had studied hard to know all the answers he was sure he would be asked. But had he studied hard enough? He had long ago stopped calling on the spirits and had given his witch-doctor's paraphernalia to Pastor Citwala. Taking this step had not been easy. In a way he almost felt as though he were parting with a special friend whom he had known and trusted all his life.

"Are you doing the right thing?" Satan tempted. "Maybe you've made a mistake." But Bonipa had learned to recognize who prompted such thoughts, and he resolutely repelled them. "Oh, Jesus," he prayed. "I know I have not made a mistake. I believe; help my unbelief."

The day of Bonipa's examination for baptism soon came and the gong clanged for the people to assemble in the large thatched area where the meetings were held. Bonipa joined the people as they made their way to the meeting place. After finding a wooden bench on which to sit, he sat down and waited with eager expectancy to see the man who would examine him.

Soon Pastor Citwala appeared, followed by the lay preacher, then Pastor Zhou.

"So this is the man who is going to ask me the questions," Bonipa thought to himself. He listened carefully to what Pastor Zhou had to say. His words carried conviction. "Surely this man speaks the truth," Bonipa remarked to the man sitting next to him.

"Aye, aye," the man agreed.

Later Pastor Zhou spoke with Bonipa alone. As he questioned him about his understanding of the Bible teachings and his love for God, he concluded that Bonipa was a sincere seeker for truth and that he was ready for baptism.

"Yes, you may be baptized," he assured Bonipa at the end of their visit. Bonipa was overjoyed.

The day before Bonipa's baptism, Pastor Zhou asked him to dress in the clothes he used to wear as a witch doctor. "It will be the last time you will ever wear them, and when you take them off, it will be symbolic of the change that has taken place in your life since you put on the robe of Christ's righteousness."

Bonipa agreed to Pastor Zhou's suggestion. At the appointed time he entered the large thatched meeting area wearing his distinctive witch-doctor's headdress, its long black feathers fluttering in the breeze, and his black cotton tunic overlaid with a grass skirt tied around his waist. In his hand he carried a carved walking stick.

He took his place with Pastor Zhou beside a table on which he had placed his witch-doctor's gear—the little tin can with the mirror and string, the kudu horn filled with medicine, and the little silver bell with which he used to call the spirits.

As Bonipa stood there, surrounded with the tools of his former craft, he put on the hardened expression he had worn for so many years as a witch doctor.

Turning to one of his helpers, Pastor Zhou instructed that a fire be lighted. Then he appealed, "I want each of you to pick out something that has been an idol to you, wrap it in a piece of paper, bring it forward, and throw it into the fire. God does not want any idol to stand between you and Him. So, get rid of your idols—those things that until now have meant more to you than the God of heaven. Get rid of the idols that connect you with the world of evil spirits. Bring them all to the fire."

The fire was lighted, and as it blazed up the people brought their idols as Pastor Zhou had instructed, and threw them in. Pastor Zhou prayed for each individual as his idol was thrown into the flames.

Picking up his little tin can with the mirror and the string, his kudu horn filled with medicine, and his little bell for calling the spirits, Bonipa led the others in throwing his former idols into the flames.

Before leaving the campgrounds, Bonipa turned over to Pastor Zhou his remaining witchcraft trappings—his headdress and grass skirt. "Please take these," he urged. "I don't want them anymore."

Soon after returning to the mission headquarters Pastor Zhou found Paul and told him he had a box for him. Paul guessed right away what it contained.

"You brought back a witch-doctor's things from your recent trip, didn't you?"

Pastor Zhou nodded.

"That's terrific! I'll go over to your house and pick up the box right away!" Paul volunteered.

When Paul returned home that evening with the witch-doctor's gear, he was ecstatic. "Whoopee! Judy! Boys! Come see what I've got!"

Paul placed the box in the middle of the dining-room table. Jeff and Greg came running to see what their father's excitement was all about. Judy heard the enthusiastic exclamations and hurried to see what was causing all the commotion. To say she was considerably less ecstatic than were Paul and the boys when she glimpsed what was in the box, is an understatement.

Not wanting to dampen the enthusiasm of the rest of the family, she said nothing at first. But after a while she asked, "What's in the box?"—as if she didn't already know.

"I just got this witch-doctor's headdress, skirt, and drums from Pastor Zhou this morning," Paul explained excitedly. "He got them from a former witch doctor named Bonipa who was recently baptized. Just imagine, Judy, how impressed the people in our churches in North America will be when they see me dressed up in these things and realize they once belonged to a witch doctor!"

Dust flew everywhere as Paul pulled out of the box a small, dark-brown drum with a well-worn goat-skin drumhead.

Judy sneezed. "Wouldn't it be a good idea to take these things outside and dust them off before bringing them into the house?" she suggested.

Apparently Paul didn't hear Judy's suggestion, for he began bringing something else out of the box.

"Look at these bones!" He exclaimed as he fingered them. "Just look at the carvings on them!" he enthused.

Putting the bones on the table, he drew out another drum, larger than the first. Eight-year-old Jeff began beating a tattoo on its light-colored top.

Paul handed four-year-old Greg a handmade tambourine. Its copper disks jingled out a pleasant patter as Greg marched around the dining-room table, shaking the instrument, while Jeff pounded on the drum.

"Is this all?" asked Judy as she tried to see what else might be in the box.

"The best till last!" chortled Paul as he produced the headdress of shining black feathers.

Judy groaned.

"Put it on, Dad! Put it on!" shouted Jeff between drum beats.

Shouts of laughter filled the room when Paul donned his new "hat" and paraded around the table for all to see. Even the servants, standing discreetly in the background, smiled.

Just then Paul caught sight of himself in the hall mirror. When he saw his reflection, he looked so ridiculous that he doubled over with laughter. As he did so, little Greg reached up and pulled the headgear off his head, to the amusement of everyone.

"Hey, be careful with that!" Paul's voice was serious now. This was no laughing matter. "These are special things, boys. We must take good care of them."

"Why don't we put them out in the garage?" Judy suggested, almost pleadingly.

"I have a better suggestion," countered Paul. "There's space high up in our bedroom cupboard. Out in the garage these things could get tossed around and ruined, or they might even get stolen. After all, this is valuable stuff."

"Did you say 'our bedroom'?" Judy questioned, then continued. "Paul, you mean you're thinking of putting that dusty old stuff in our bedroom?"

"That's the best place I can think of—unless you want to store it in the kitchen?" Paul teased.

Judy knew Paul well enough to realize that no amount of arguing was going to make him change his mind once he'd made it up. So she reconciled herself to storing the witch-doctor's gear in their bedroom.

"But," she insisted, "before you put them in the bedroom, at least take them outside and dust them off."

"Gladly!" Paul agreed, and with the boys' eager help the task was quickly accomplished.

Busy days slipped into weeks, and Judy all but forgot about the box in the bedroom cupboard—until one eventful night. Paul was leaving for a three-week trip to Botswana the next morning. They had stayed up longer than usual in order to finish packing Paul's bags for his trip. He would be meeting many literature evangelists for the first time, and he was eager to present all the right materials to inspire them in their work.

When at last his bags were packed, Paul turned out the light and crawled into bed. It didn't take him long to drift off to sleep.

Suddenly Paul clutched at the bedcovers. At first it seemed to him as though he were dreaming. But he'd never had a dream like this. He tried to scream but couldn't. Rousing to semi-consciousness, he lashed out at "someone" who was grabbing him, trying to choke him. "Help me! Help me!" he yelled, but no help came. Finally his "screams" broke through his sleep-filled brain, and he suddenly realized he wasn't dreaming at all. Someone *was* trying to strangle him!

Paul tried to scream for help, but his words were strangled by the hands that gripped his throat like a vise. He pulled at the hands and thrashed wildly at his assailant who held him down on the bed.

He fought to sit up but was thrown back hard onto the bed.

About this time the commotion wakened Judy, who

concluded that a thief had broken into the house.

"They're trying to kill Paul!" she thought wildly. "Get out!" she screamed. "Leave him alone!" she yelled. But the wrestling didn't stop. Paul continued fighting with the intruder—who was obviously very strong. Although Judy could not see him, his presence seemed to fill the darkened room.

Shouting frantically Judy grabbed a shoe and flung it with all her might at the intruder just as Paul was picked up bodily and hurled back onto the bed. Fumbling along the wall, she tried to inch her way toward the light switch.

Meanwhile Paul tried to fling the bed covers over the intruder's head with one hand while pushing him away with the other. Struggling desperately he managed to force his way toward the door, where the light switch was located. Reaching out, he touched the switch. The instant before he flipped it, the choking stopped and his assailant fled.

Light now flooded the room. Paul peered down the hall, but the "man" was nowhere to be seen. Where had he gone? How had he escaped? One thing was certain, he couldn't have gone far.

Dashing out into the hallway, Paul and Judy were met by Jeff and Greg, who had been awakened by the commotion. "Which way did he go?" demanded Paul.

Jeff looked confused. "Where did *who* go?" he asked in bewilderment.

"The man!" yelled Judy. "Didn't you see a man come running down the hall? Where did he go?"

"I didn't see anyone," replied Jeff, his eyes beginning to fill with terror. "I just heard you screaming and woke up."

Greg looked up into his mother's frightened face, and tears began trickling down his cheeks as he sensed his parents' panic.

Paul ran back into the bedroom, sure that if the "man" hadn't bolted down the hall, he must be hiding in there somewhere. He looked frantically under the bed and in the closet, but he could see no one. He checked the entrances to the bedroom. The windows were all closed, and there was no other way into the bedroom, other than the door.

Bewildered, Paul again walked down the hallway. In the meantime Judy turned on all the lights in the house. "That scoundrel has to be in here somewhere!" she declared.

Although the couple considered every possibility they could think of, there was no way the intruder could have entered or left the house without leaving some evidence of his presence. Just to make sure, they rechecked all the windows and doors. The front door was locked securely. The same was true of the back door. All the windows were securely shut—just the way they had left them when they went to bed that night. They again searched the whole house, but could find nothing.

Back in the bedroom Judy glanced at Paul's neck. "Just look at your neck!" she exclaimed. "You have finger marks all over your throat! That wicked man must have intended to kill you."

After bedding down the boys once more and staying with them until they were asleep, Paul and Judy returned to their own bedroom, where they knelt and prayed, asking God for protection during the remainder of the night.

As they climbed into bed Paul reached for the light switch, but Judy stopped him. "Please, Paul, let's leave the lights on," she pleaded. "I don't think the intruder will dare come back if we leave them on." It didn't take much coaxing to persuade Paul.

Before long, Paul, exhausted by his struggle with

the mysterious intruder, was fast asleep. Not Judy. She lay wide awake, the bed covers pulled up over her mouth, with only the upper part of her head exposed. She felt afraid to move a muscle, and her heart pounded wildly. Over and over her imagination replayed the terrifying struggle that had just taken place.

As she pondered what had happened, Judy's mind drifted back to her childhood—memories of her parents' tragic death in a train crash, the people who had reared her, the relatives and friends she had known. Out of the dark recesses of her memory rang the words, "Watch out, Judy! Although your parents are dead, the devil can come back looking just like them. Watch out! The devil is very sly, you know." These words tormented her like a monotonous, clattering gong.

Because of words like these, Judy instinctively feared anything having to do with the supernatural. There were times when she wondered whether or not the devil would appear to her as her parents to frighten her. She knew, of course, that God was more powerful than Satan, but the words spoken to her when she was a child had their disquieting effect.

"Could the 'man' who attacked Paul have been the devil?" she wondered. The more she relived the struggle that night, the more she was convinced that the intruder was one of Satan's evil angels.

A strange feeling of apprehension filled her heart as she thought of Paul's leaving the next day for his trip to Botswana.

"How can I endure three weeks without him in this house?" she worried. "If it was the devil, will he follow where Paul goes, or will he stay here?"

As her thoughts turned to the only One who can defeat Satan, Psalm 34:7 came to her mind: "The angel of the Lord encampeth round about them that fear him, and delivereth them." Through the sleepless hours that dragged slowly by that night, she clung to these comforting words. She repeated them over and over until the rays of the morning sun slowly scattered the gloom of night.

"If the intruder was one of Satan's angels, what could have brought about this encounter?" she wondered.

Next morning Judy thought about expressing her apprehension to Paul, but after thinking it over decided against it. She felt sure he would play down the incident and explain her apprehension as the product of an overworked imagination. She could just hear him saying, "Why, Judy, we're Christians. We believe in Jesus, and no devil would dare come into *our* house." So she said nothing.

That morning during the union office worship, Paul related his experience to his fellow workers. He showed them the finger marks on his throat and said, "That fellow was quick. Believe it or not, by the time I turned on the lights he was gone!"

The workers began talking all at once, one suggesting this solution, another that. Finally one pastor spoke up and said, "It sounds like the devil to me. I've seen too much of his work here in Africa to dismiss this incident lightly." He paused, then asked Paul, "Is it true that Pastor Zhou recently gave you some tools from an ex–witch doctor?"

"Yes," Paul replied.

"Where did you put them?" he questioned.

"I put them in a cupboard in our bedroom." A look of sudden realization crossed Paul's face. Why hadn't he thought of that before? "You don't think . . . ?" he stammered but didn't finish.

"I would recommend that you take those things out of your room," the worker advised.

When Paul returned home to pick up his bags for his trip, he instructed one of the servants to remove the box with the witch-doctor's paraphernalia from his bedroom and put it out in the garage. The servant complied.

"Now everything will be all right," Paul assured Judy. "Don't worry about me. God will protect both of us, I know." Giving his wife a kiss, he hurried out the door for his three-week itinerary.

Notwithstanding these assurances, Judy remained apprehensive. As darkness crept over the town Judy made sure she wasn't alone in the house. She brought in the family's two dogs, her children, and the servants. Then she turned on all the lights, indoors as well as the ones outside. This done, she organized her household to protect them against another "intruder." Greg and Jeff were bedded down in her bedroom, the dogs were made to lie on the floor beside her bed, and the servants were instructed to sleep in the hallway. Judy then opened her Bible to Psalm 34:7 and placed it on her night stand and prepared for bed.

It was very late when Judy finally drifted off into a fitful, uneasy sleep that first night. Several times she awoke with a feeling of apprehension and checked to see if everything was all right. It was, but it was a relief when morning finally came.

Judy's little ritual of preparation was repeated every night while Paul was gone. When she wasn't worrying about herself and the boys, she worried about Paul. Was he all right? Was the devil after him? By now he had been gone over a week, and she had received no word from him.

One evening as Judy tucked the children into bed the telephone rang. Judy ran to answer it.

"Hello. Judy? This is Paul."

At the sound of her husband's voice tears welled up in her eyes and streamed down her cheeks. "Paul, are you all right?" she asked, choking back the tears.

"Yes, yes, everything's fine. And you?"

"I'm much better now knowing that you are all right. But I have been worried. The nights are dreadful without you," she rushed on, wanting to pour out all her pent-up words at once. She'd only had the children to talk to, and she didn't want to frighten them, so she had maintained a calm exterior with a reassuring smile. But underneath she was churning with tensions.

Paul's steady voice and enthusiasm for his work calmed and reassured his wife, and she hoped that the remaining days of separation would be easier to endure.

Two weeks later Paul arrived at home. That night, for the first time in three weeks, the dogs were put outside, the children returned to their own bedrooms, and the servants went to their own sleeping quarters in the rooms adjoining the garage.

"Have you kept the lights on all night while I've been gone?" questioned Paul with a grin.

Judy nodded. "How else did you expect me to get any rest?"

"With the lights out!" Paul teased, reaching for the switch and turning it off. "Everything will be all right now," said Paul, trying to inspire his wife with confidence. "The witch-doctor's things are out of the house now, so we won't be bothered anymore. Everything will be all right, I'm sure."

That night, while things seemed to be quiet and peaceful in the house, strange things were going on out in the servants' sleeping quarters. Although they didn't say much, they did report the next morning that they had gotten very little sleep.

About two weeks later Paul rose earlier than usual and strolled out into the back yard. He observed that the servants were rolled up in their blankets, stretched out on the grass, fast asleep in one corner of the yard.

"This is strange," Paul mused.

It wasn't long before the servants were up and dressed, ready for work. As Mai Edi came into the kitchen to wash the dishes Paul asked her, "I notice that you and the other servants are sleeping outside. Are your mattresses no good?"

"Oh no, Bwana," she answered respectfully. "The beds you bought us—they very good. But . . ." she hesitated as though afraid tell him the real reason.

Paul encouraged her to continue.

"It's just that . . . well . . . it's the spirits, Bwana."

"The spirits?" Paul queried.

Mai Edi continued, her dark eyes reflecting terror, "The spirits—they try to strangle *us,* Bwana. Ever since you came back from your trip we have been sleeping on the grass away from the garage. Yes, the spirits have been coming every night. It is terrible! To get away from them we take our blankets and go outside to sleep—far away from the garage. The spirits don't bother us there."

"I wonder if it could be the witch-doctor's things?" Paul thought. He remembered he had them stored in the garage, thinking to get rid of their evil influence, but obviously, whatever it was had gone with them to the garage.

Mai Edi confirmed what Paul had been thinking. "I think that the trouble is that box with the witch-doctor's things. No one plays with a *nyangas* (witch-doctor) things without being troubled by the spirits. We Africans know. The spirits go wherever the witch-doctor's things go." She hesitated. "But I see you like that box. You want to keep those things, no?"

Paul nodded. But he was beginning to question the wisdom of having such things around his home.

Mai Edi continued. "What can we do?" The servant girl spread her hands apart in resignation. "If you keep them—we sleep outside." She turned to the sink and began rinsing the dishes.

Judy entered the kitchen just then, having over-heard the last of the servant's remarks. "Get rid of that box, Paul," she pleaded. "Those things are filled with the devil. I know they are. And to think we keep them on *our* premises. Please get rid of them."

"But, Judy . . . ," Paul began to rationalize. He stopped short. He knew his wife was right. No matter how much he wanted to keep the witch-doctor's things, he knew down deep they belonged to the devil. And yet, he wanted to keep them so he could show them off in the homeland. Torn between what he wanted and what he knew he should do, he said no more.

Just then the kitchen clock sounded its chime.

"I'm late for work. I've got to go. I'll see what I can do," he promised, grabbing his jacket. After giving Judy a quick kiss, he ran out the door, got into his car, and drove away.

Paul returned that evening, his footsteps sounding light and eager on the walkway. Judy heard him and ran to the door.

"Judy, I believe we have the answer to the witch-doctor's things. I've been talking to Pastor Joe Hunt, who suggested we 'baptize' them."

"Baptize them?" Judy looked puzzled. "What do you mean, 'baptize them'?"

Paul smiled at the mystified look on Judy's face.

"I don't mean baptize them the way we usually use the word. I mean dedicate the witch-doctor's things to God and His glory. After all, isn't that what baptism means? Joe is coming over this evening. Let's bring out the witch-doctor's things and be ready for him, when he arrives."

Together Paul and Judy went to the garage and pulled down the tattered box.

That evening Pastor Hunt arrived. As soon as he entered the house Judy felt assurance that God was in control. Here was a man who allowed the power of God to work through him. Judy and Paul opened the box with the former witch-doctor's tools.

"We need to 'baptize' these things by dedicating them to God," he explained. "When we do, God can make the evil spirits flee. We won't use water for this kind of baptism. We will simply pray."

Laying out the witch-doctor's things on the table—the drums and bones, the tambourine and the feathered headdress—they knelt in prayer. Pastor Hunt pleaded that God would make the evil spirits leave and let the Cordray home rest in peace.

"We wish to consecrate these things to you, O Father," he prayed, "these things that Bonipa used in his practice of witchcraft, these things that Bonipa has forsaken, so that he could follow You. We dedicate them to You, O God. May it be known by all who see them that You, dear God, are more powerful than the evil spirits. May Your name be glorified, when others see that Your power can overcome the devil. Let others know that You are working in a mighty way, changing people's lives, bringing peace where once was unrest and turmoil, bringing joy where once was sorrow, lighting people's faces with the illumination of Your Spirit. Thank You, Lord, for Your almighty power evidenced in the quiet working of Your love, and in the marvelous manifestations that thrill every part of our being. May these bones and drums, feathers and tambourine be used to glorify *You,* and no one else, O God. And to this end I now baptize them in the name of the Father, and of the Son, and of the Holy Ghost. Amen."

A new peace permeated the missionaries' home, a peace that remained long after Pastor Hunt had gone. Paul put the witch-doctor's things back into the box again and placed it on the shelf in the garage. Never again did they cause any more trouble.

If you should ask Paul today about his faith in the greatness of God, he would tell you that God is greater than all the witch doctors in Africa. Never for a moment does he doubt God's power. Whenever he displays the witch-doctor's paraphernalia, God, not he, gets the glory. Whether God's love is revealed in the quiet ways that we have to search for, or whether it is displayed in the miraculous overthrow of the devil's power, there is no doubt with Paul that God lives and is greater than the forces of evil!

Chapter 2
God Sent the Doctor

The rainy season was just a few weeks away. The grass was tinder dry. All it would take was a spark to set the hills on fire. Every day the villagers swept clean the hard-packed dirt around their thatch-roofed huts. They didn't want a fire in their village.

Farai's mother took special care to light her cooking fire. She didn't use any more sticks than necessary. But it had to be a hot fire for cooking. With patience borne of experience she fanned the sparks into a flame. Quickly she placed the long-handled black pot over the fire, supported by surrounding rocks, then she watched the water in the pot come to a boil. After a bit she added white meal and stirred it vigorously. Minutes passed, as she stirred and the porridge thickened. As soon as it was the proper consistency she removed it from the fire, then turned to place the pot on a nearby stone.

While her back was turned little Farai toddled across the hard-packed dirt. Walking unsteadily on his chubby little legs he walked toward Mother and the fire. Closer and closer he toddled, unknown to Mother, who was busy fixing dinner.

Suddenly a scream of pain pierced the air. Mother turned and with horrified eyes saw Farai wedged between two rocks, his feet kicking the air wildly and his hand in the middle of the blazing fire.

She grabbed him up, his loud wailing alerting the neighbors, who came running from every direction. Taking one look at Farai's charred arm and hand they cried, "Take him to the hospital!"

Carrying her screaming child, Mother hurried as fast as she could to the local hospital. It was a long walk away. She arrived panting and tired while Farai continued his painful cries. The nurse attending was sympathetic, but she had no special medicine for burns. She gave Farai a pill to take away the pain. Then she cleaned and bandaged the ugly wounds. Giving Mother some more medicine, she sent them home with instructions to return in a few days.

For days Farai wore his bandage as he toddled around the yard. He cried constantly and he ate little. He grew sicker and sicker. It was so very far to the hospital. In distress Mother went to Chambo Seventh-day Adventist Clinic near her village.

It just happened (or did it just happen?) that Dr. Tom Shepherd was making a visit to Chambo Clinic that day. It had been nearly two months since he last made the long, dusty trip way up over the mountains to see how the well-trained staff were getting along.

As he was counseling with the staff, in walked Mother, carrying a very sick-looking boy. Gently the nurse unwound the soiled bandage from Farai's arm and hand. He was too weak to protest the pain when it was uncovered. An ugly, unhealed burn met their eyes. Puss drained profusely from the swollen area.

Dr. Shepherd thought, "He's going to lose his hand if something isn't done soon."

"We don't have the proper medicine here," said the nurse sorrowfully. "What shall we do?"

Everyone quietly thought a moment. "Rhumpi

Hospital," Dr. Shepherd said out loud. "They have the proper medicine there."

"But Rhumpi is so far away!" the nurses protested. "Many miles away! And the roads are terrible! Surely there's some place closer."

But try as they might, they could not think of any place closer where Farai could receive the treatment he needed. Dr. Shepherd looked at his watch. "It will take about seven hours to get there. If this little boy is going to keep his hand we had better get started."

Piling Mother and Farai into his four-wheel Daihatsu, Dr. Shepherd started off on the long, long journey. Every hour was vital.

Up the hills to the top of the plateau Dr. Shepherd drove as fast as he could, bumping along over the dusty roads. Down the other side and into the humid lakeshore land. Inside, Mother held Farai tenderly in her arms, softening the bumps for her whimpering sick boy. Hour after hour bumped by as they drove the many miles. Dr. Shepherd prayed that it wasn't too late to save Farai's infected hand.

Finally they reached Rhumpi Hospital. Attendants greeted them and hurried Farai into the treatment room. Dr. Shepherd sighed. Seven hours of driving were behind him. Now he could relax.

Next morning he was on his way again, visiting other clinics and attending to needs in other parts of the country.

Months went by. It was time to visit Chambo Clinic again. Dr. Shepherd had nearly forgotten the incident of Farai and his burned hand. Arriving at the clinic, a woman excitedly greeted him.

"Do you remember me?" she asked. "Do you remember him?" She pointed to the smiling child sitting on her lap. Without letting Dr. Shepherd answer, she eagerly continued, "This is Farai. You saved his hand. At the hospital far away they made his hand all well again. Look!" She held up his arm and hand for all to see.

Sure enough it didn't look like the same hand of two months before. It was so well healed that very few scars could be seen. Dr. Shepherd took the boy's small hand in his. A broad smile of delight brightened his face as he looked into Farai's eager eyes. "I'm glad we made that long journey. Farai is happy too, I can see."

Before Dr. Shepherd left Chambo Clinic that day, Mother ran up the trail carrying a large stalk of bananas on her head. She laid them at Dr. Shepherd's feet and bowed in respect.

"Thank you. Thank you, Doctor," she said. "Without you Farai would not be well today."

Dr. Shepherd turned to the mother and said, "It was not me. It was the loving God in heaven who sent me here to Chambo the very day you came to the clinic. And it was God who made your little boy well. You can thank God."

Loading the gift of bananas into his Daihatsu, Dr. Shepherd bade Farai and his mother goodbye and started back down the dusty road. As he drove away he couldn't help but marvel at God's great wisdom. "Even in the everyday events of life God intervenes to reveal His power," he thought. "Some may call it happenstance; others call it luck. But I have no doubt that it was God. For God is greater than all the luck the world will ever know."

Mother watched wistfully as Dr. Shepherd's vehicle drove into the distance, dust swirling around its wheels. "Thank you, God," she whispered. "Thank you for sending the doctor."

Chapter 3
Behind Prison Doors

Pastor Matambo gripped the steering wheel of his car tighter as he approached the police roadblock. Reports had been circulating for some time of unwarranted arrests for no apparent reason. Pastor Matambo breathed a silent prayer for protection as he pulled over and stopped. He forced a cheery Hello, but the patrolmen did not return the greeting.

Without so much as a glimmer of recognition the officers ordered, "Out!" and yanked open the car door. Pastor Matambo stood to his feet. He was surrounded at once. One officer grabbed his shirt, another his tie, others yanked off his shoes. Pulling the keys from his car, they marched him off to jail. Pastor Matambo's pleas for mercy fell on unlistening ears.

When they reached the prison, the officers pushed him roughly into a cell with iron bars, locked the gate, and disappeared. Panic seized the pastor as the helplessness of his situation dawned on him. Here he was locked up with over 300 other prisoners with no prospects of fair trial or release.

His sudden arrest without warning worried him. Who would know what had happened to him and where he was? Certainly his wife and family would have no idea he had been arrested and was in jail.

Then suddenly Pastor Matambo remembered the

women—the church women who came every day, bringing food for the prisoners. Why, of course. He would tell them of his arrest, and they would notify his family and arrange for his release. A smile of relief tugged at the corners of his mouth.

Later that day, as he made his way through the food line, one of the women visiting the prison recognized him.

"Pastor Matambo!" she exclaimed. "What are you doing here? Your wife is worried about you." A shadow crossed her face as she handed him a dish of food. "Due to the turmoil in our country, it is very difficult to get prisoners released," she said quietly. "But I will notify the mission office, and we shall be praying for you."

Pastor Matambo thanked the woman and added, "Please bring me a Bible. Everything was taken from me when I was brought here. If only I can have a Bible I can endure anything."

Pastor Matambo looked around him and saw other men who also had no hope of release from prison, but who, unlike him, had no knowledge of a Saviour who could release them from their prison house of sin. So, as soon as he obtained a Bible, he began a Bible class. Only one prisoner listened at first. But as the days lengthened into weeks, more men gathered around him anxious to hear the words of life. Eagerly they listened and discussed the subjects presented.

Pastor Matambo prayed for each man, longing to see the men accept Jesus as their Saviour. In fact, he became so involved in his Bible studies that before he realized it a month had passed.

Then one day it was announced that the prison inspector was coming, and all the prisoners were ordered to bathe and dress in clean clothes. The prisoners were glad to comply. They were thankful for the chance to wash the accumulating dirt from their hair and bodies.

When the inspector arrived, the prisoners all lined up for inspection. Yelling his orders for all to hear, he carried out his inspection routine, his gruff voice demanding respect.

"I know that man!" thought Pastor Matambo suddenly as the inspector arrogantly strode about the room. "I know I've been to his office on business. I wonder if he will remember me. And, if he does, will he work on my release?" Hope sent his heart racing excitedly. Silently he prayed.

The inspector stood for a moment, casually running his eyes along the line of prisoners. Suddenly his gaze stopped. He looked directly at Pastor Matambo. A sudden look of recognition crossed his face. "Is that you, Pastor Matambo?" he asked, a note of concern softening the roughness in his manner.

"Yes, I am Pastor Matambo," he answered politely, hoping against hope that the inspector might set him free.

Turning to the guard beside him, the inspector commanded, "Release this man immediately! He should not be here." Then he added, "Return everything that has been taken from him." With a twinkle in his eye he looked at the pastor once more, then turned abruptly and left the room.

All at once the men crowded around Pastor Matambo. "Ask for my release," begged one. "And mine too," pleaded another. The men who had been attending the pastor's Bible class said, "We shall miss you, pastor. What shall we do without you? You have taught us so much. Since you came, we have found a hope we never knew before. Please come back and visit us."

Pastor Matambo assured them that he would return and continue studying with them. He would not forget them. How could he? Thirty-two of those prisoners were now ready for baptism! No, he would never forget them. He would return.

Within an hour Pastor Matambo's shirt, tie, shoes, and his car were all returned to him. When he reached home, his family rejoiced in the knowledge that God is greater than all the plans of men. Greater than locked prison doors or man-made laws.

God's greatness was now seen by all the men in the prison, not only the prisoners, but the guards and the officers as well. Pastor Matambo has come to believe firmly that "all things [do] work together for good to them that love God." Romans 8:28. His faith was strengthened as he experienced this demonstration that God lives and intervenes on behalf of His servants.

Chapter 4
Prison Doors Unlocked

The heavily guarded door clanged shut behind me, its finality echoing off the barren walls. I walked through the prison corridor, a guard at my side, until we came to a second door. This one was secured with locks and bolts. The guard fumbled with his large ring of keys, found the right one, and inserted it into the lock. The lock turned, opening the door to yet another empty corridor. I stepped inside; the guard followed. The large door banged shut behind us, shattering the eerie silence.

We walked on, tension mounting within me at every step. "Will I ever get back through these doors again, back to the outside world?" I wondered. We walked on and came to a third door, then a fourth.

I tried to make small talk with my guard to lessen my nervousness. But his dark face gave no sign of comprehension; his countenance remained expression-less. He seemed to be concentrating all his attention on his keys and on every fortified door.

Finally, the last door swung open on squeaky hinges, and I found myself standing in a small room with only a tiny barred window to break the monotony of its cold walls.

The guard who had silently accompanied me finally

found his voice and barked out, "Only fifteen minutes!"

I stood uncertainly, waiting for the man I had come to see—a man I did not know, a man who was a prisoner in this maximum-security prison. "Would my visit do this man any good?" I wondered. As I waited, I recalled the events which had brought me here.

Early Friday evening my telephone had rung, bringing the request that I visit Henry.

"His oldest brother has just died," the caller explained, "and the family requests that a Seventh-day Adventist minister visit Henry in prison to break the sad news to him."

My mind raced with excuses: "Why me? I've had no experience with prisoners. In fact, I've never before even been inside a prison!" But sensing that God had a reason in this request, I agreed to go, saying, "I will try to make contact with him as soon as possible."

I did not know how difficult this request would be until I had phoned the prison authorities that evening and my request was met with a curt, "Sir, it is simply not possible for you to visit the prisoner. Our prison chaplain is capable of conveying your message to him."

Undaunted, I had spoken to one officer after the other, explaining my mission. Praying earnestly, I finally spoke to the highest officer in charge. There was a long pause after I had stated the purpose of my visit. I waited, wondering whom I'd have to call next, if my request was denied.

The officer hesitated as he spoke. "Come tomorrow—tomorrow afternoon at 2:45. We'll take you—to Henry." I thanked the officer with a sigh of grateful relief.

And now here I was, standing in the middle of the maximum-security section of the prison, behind six locked doors, waiting to see Henry, a hardened criminal—a man I had never seen before.

As I mentioned before, my accompanying guard stood silent. A feeling of annoyance seemed to exude from him. I directed my attention to the small square window before me, feeling impatient with the delay as the seconds slowly ticked by.

Then suddenly I heard him coming, shuffling his way toward the window. A guard followed close behind him. Finally Henry made his appearance. His face was expressionless. He wore no smile or frown that might give me a clue as to his thoughts or feelings. Motionless, he stood waiting in front of the window, his eyes not meeting mine.

"I am a Seventh-day Adventist minister," I began. "A friend of your family has asked me to visit you." Slowly, prayerfully, I told him the reason for my visit, expressing sympathy for the loss of his brother and expressing words of comfort. I paused, hoping for some reaction.

Slowly his eyes lifted, meeting mine straight on. Gripping the small table in front of him he spoke, his voice trembling with emotion, "Thank you, Padre." He seemed to want to say more, but no words came—only three short words were all he spoke.

I prayed for him, my silent guard standing by my side, hearing every word. I pleaded for God to comfort Henry and for God to become an important part of his life. Though we were separated by glass and bars I felt a closeness to the prisoner that locks and doors could never separate.

On my way out of the prison I gave my accompanying guard six pieces of literature, requesting that he give these to Henry. He took them without saying a word, and I couldn't help wondering if Henry would ever see them.

Weeks went by. I could not get Henry out of my thoughts—or my prayers. Then, six weeks after my visit, I received a letter from Henry. Excitedly I tore it open. In scrawled handwriting, he expressed gratitude for my visit.

"I had been praying for someone to visit me from the world outside," he wrote. "The other men and I have read every word of the magazines you gave me. Please, do you have more?"

Feeling elated, I asked to visit Henry again. This time I was readily given permission. As I made my way through the locked doors, the attending guard seemed less annoyed by my presence this time. And when I met Henry, his face was wreathed in smiles.

It wasn't long before the prison chaplain heard about my visits. The prisoners had commented so favorably about the literature I had brought Henry that they begged him to get more. Knowing how much the prisoners enjoyed singing, the chaplain contacted me, asking if our church could donate song books in the local language for the prisoners. I was more than delighted!

The day I delivered the hymnals, I was filled with eager anticipation. At the appointed time, I entered the chaplain's office. To my surprise, I was met by Henry and twenty other prisoners. Eagerly they came forward, expressing their thanks and praising God for having sent me to visit them. Tears welled up in my eyes as I listened to songs of praise from these condemned men. Although they were locked behind heavy bars and countless doors, they sang praises to their new-found freedom in God.

Henry's life began to change. It wasn't long before he accepted Jesus as his personal Saviour. The prison superintendent personally testified to the change in many of the prisoners' lives since I had begun visiting and leaving literature. He had nothing but praise for the work of the Seventh-day Adventists.

"I personally request that you apply for a prison pass so that you and others from your church can visit as often as you like," he said.

I gratefully acknowledged his support and thanked God for using me in His plan for a prison ministry in this city.

Currently Henry is studying the books *Your Bible and You* and *Bible Readings for the Home*. Recently he was transferred to the low-security prison area due to his exemplary behavior.

I am glad I can work for a God who is greater than locked doors or hardened criminals. I am thankful our God is able to open doors to criminals in the prison house of sin, restcring them to the liberty of the gospel and making them whole.

Chapter 5
Two Cockroaches

Joseph Muganda struggled awake. Rubbing his eyes he sat up, peering around the darkened bedroom, wondering what had awakened him. Then he remembered—a dream. That's what had awakened him.

But what was the dream about? He sat tense, trying to pull the images back into his memory. "It seemed so important. And it had seemed so real! What was it about?" His mind whirled, trying to recall it. Slowly snatches appeared in his mind's eye—a book . . . a bookseller . . . something to read.

"That's it!" Now he remembered it clearly. It all came back in a rush. It was a dream about a book, a large brown book, the book he had bought from a man who had come to the door many months before.

The book salesman's talk had sounded so good at the time that he bought his book, intending to use it for sermon material, for preparing his sermons for his Lutheran church members. But somehow, after the salesman had gone Joseph had never opened the book again. He had placed it on the shelf and promptly forgot all about it.

But now, months later, he was reminded again of that book—in a dream. In his dream, he recalled, someone had spoken very distinctly to him. Pointing to the book, a man had commanded, "Read that book! Read it all!"

The dream had been as clear as a well-developed picture. There was no mistaking the book the person told him to read. "I wonder what can be so important about that book?" he mused.

As he thought about it, his curiosity was aroused, so much so that even though it was the middle of the night, he got out of bed and walked over to the bookcase and looked for the book.

Although he could not remember its title, he was sure he would know it when he saw it.

As he searched along the shelf, a wave of terror flooded over him. "What if I don't find it? What if it's not here? How will I ever know what important message it has? How will I know why I had this dream? I *must* find it. It *has* to be here!"

In desperation Joseph searched the bookcase, quickly scanning one book, then another, until he came to the end of the long shelf. Only one book left. It was far back on the shelf. There, pushed into the neglected corner of the shelf stood a large brown book, its binding new and shining. "This is the book I saw in my dream," he whispered excitedly.

With eager hands Joseph pulled it from its hiding place and read the title: *The Great Controversy.* "Yes, now I remember," he murmured, as he held the book in his trembling hands.

He remembered the salesman saying, "This book has a very important message in it. Read it all, because it even tells what will happen in the future. "

Opening the smooth brown cover, Joseph began to read. Easing himself down into a nearby chair, he read on and on, oblivious to the passing of time. Dawn found him still entranced by the book, unable to put it down. All other assignments were pushed aside as he eagerly read through the day. New and strange ideas came into his mind as he read, and when he finished the book, his mind reeled in confusion.

The following days found Joseph at his desk, pouring over the Bible and this strange new book. "How can this be true?" he questioned time and again. "Why have I never heard this before? Why did the professors at the Lutheran seminary never mention these things in class? Is it possible that this book is simply someone's imaginings?"

But every time he tried to refute the book's statements with a Bible text, he came up short. He was especially perplexed about the seventh day being God's holy rest day, called in the Bible the Sabbath. Over and over he studied the book and the Bible texts, hoping to prove his conviction to be wrong. But the more he studied, the more he became convinced that the seventh-day Sabbath was the day men are to keep and that there was no proof for Sunday keeping.

The next Sunday, as he preached, he fought the new ideas he had discovered. He cherished the teachings he had been taught to believe, and yet, his mind constantly darted back to the new things he had read.

As the week progressed, each day found him more and more tormented by the words of the book. Finally his frustrations reached the boiling point. Angrily grabbing the book from his desk, he flung it into the wastebasket shouting, "That's the last I want to hear about your 'Seven-day' teachings. I wish I'd never read your words! I'm done with you. I'm finished with your fanatical ideas!" So saying he stomped from the room.

Days sped into weeks—restless weeks for Joseph. For even though he tried to forget his dream and the book, it seemed that they followed him everywhere he went. Whenever Sunday arrived and he stood in the pulpit to preach, the words flashed in his mind like neon signs, "Remember the Sabbath day to keep it holy." He preached long and loud, trying to drown the conflicting thoughts.

It was after church one Sunday that his wife commented, "Joseph, you don't seem yourself these days. You appear agitated, restless. What is the matter?"

Joseph told her about the dream and the book and what he had read. "It says that Saturday is the true Sabbath, and all those who truly follow the Lord will keep that day holy." Tired anger filled his voice.

His wife, a God-fearing woman, quietly suggested, "Let's pray about it, Joseph." And they did.

Joseph felt no peace in the days that followed. His wife, seeing his continued anxiety, prayed more and more for peace in her husband's life again. Yet he struggled on through the weeks, fighting to keep his old, comfortable beliefs intact, wishing he had never seen the book or had the dream.

One morning, after an exceptionally restless night, Joseph told his wife, "I've got to know the truth! I must find out whether Sunday or Saturday is the right day to keep. I have been tormented long enough. I'm going to make a test."

"A test?" his wife questioned.

"Yes," he answered with determination. "Tonight I'm going to set two bowls of water out on the desk. I'll mark one bowl 'Sunday,' the other 'Saturday.' In the morning, if there are two cockroaches in one of the bowls, that will show me that that is not the right day to keep. The bowl without any cockroaches will be God's true holy day. That's going to be my test."

Immediately the story of Gideon and his test with the fleeces came to the wife's mind. Was her husband another Gideon, asking God for a sign? Whatever it would take to bring peace, she was willing to join her husband in. She was weary of seeing his indecision and observing its effect on him.

That evening as the two bowls were set out, Joseph and his wife knelt to pray. "Oh, God, please show me the true holy day—the true Sabbath," Joseph pleaded. "Show me the day on which we should worship You. In the morning when I come here again, if I find two cockroaches in the bowl I will know that that is *not* the true day to keep, and if the bowl is clean, I will know it is the true day of worship."

Sleep did not come easily that night! Over and over in his mind Joseph rehearsed his test: "If two cockroaches are in the Saturday bowl, I will know that the dream and the book were wrong, that it is just a scheme of the devil to confuse and mislead me. But if the cockroaches are in the Sunday bowl. . ." His thoughts raced on.

"Is it possible. . . ?" his thoughts trailed off. "How could so many churches and ministers be wrong? Surely God changed the seventh-day Sabbath to Sunday. Surely Sunday is the Lord's day. And yet, the Bible says the seventh day is the Sabbath. Maybe the book was right . . . maybe. . . ." And so the battle raged. It seemed that morning would never come.

At the crack of dawn Joseph was up. With his wife at his side, he walked quietly through the house to check on the bowls. As they approached his desk, there were the two bowls, exactly where he had placed them the night before. Joseph suddenly saw them! "Look!" he stammered in a hoarse whisper. "Look! Two cockroaches!" In the Sunday bowl were two cockroaches! And the other? "Yes," he said, "it is clean."

Joseph glanced from one bowl to the other and exclaimed, "It's clean! The Saturday bowl is clean. Saturday, not Sunday, *Saturday!*"

Now he was fairly shouting it—shouting in relief.

"Saturday is God's day. Saturday is the Sabbath! God has answered our prayers! God has heard us!"

Turning to his wife, Joseph put his arms around her saying, "Now we know God is the Lord of the Sabbath—Lord of the seventh day. Wife, there are many things we will have to change in our lives, but God has answered our prayers, and we can trust Him to lead us further. Let us thank Him."

As they prayed, tears streamed down their cheeks. "God," they prayed, "show us where to go from here. We will follow You wherever You lead. Even though it will not be easy to leave the church we've grown up in, the church we love; even though it will be hard to leave our friends and family, we will obey You. Please continue to guide us and lead us. Help us to proclaim your true Sabbath in whatever way You have planned for us. Please show us what You want us to do."

Suddenly a picture of the salesman standing at the door with the book in his hand flashed into Joseph's mind. As the picture came into focus, it seemed that he was the salesman! "Can this be what God wants me to do?" he wondered.

Today, Joseph Muganda, a former minister of the Lutheran church, is joyously going from door-to-door, selling books that change lives. Eagerly he tells people about his dream and about his baptism into the Seventh-day Adventist Church—the Sabbath-keeping church. He is determined to tell the whole message that God wants the world to hear. He has the unshakable conviction that God lives and is greater than all of man's teachings or preconceived ideas, and that He answers prayer.

Chapter 6
God's Umbrella

"The church doors are still locked," sighed the local African church elder, turning away from the padlocked church doors.

It had been many weeks since the police closed the church. Would they ever permit it to be opened again? Dejectedly the elder made his way to the cleared area where the church members were waiting for the services to begin.

Uppermost in their minds was the impending rainy season. They could worship God out-of-doors without much hardship during the dry months. But how could they meet together in the rain, which often poured down by the bucketful, sending everyone running for cover? They decided to make this disagreeable prospect the special subject of prayer. Kneeling together they earnestly prayed that God would open their church doors before the rains began.

Sabbath after Sabbath came and passed, but the church doors remained locked. There seemed no change in the government's attitude. With foreboding the church members watched and waited as the rainy season approached and clouds built into ominous, angry thunderheads.

While their neighbors eagerly awaited the rains

which heralded the planting season of maize and millet, the church members' faith began to grow faint. Would God answer their prayers?

Then came the Sabbath when the first large drops of rain splattered onto the ground, sending up sprays of dust from the parched earth. Hopes of productive crops filled the minds of everyone—everyone, that is, except the church members. Weighed down with disappointment, they walked past their church with its doors padlocked securely.

"Why has God not answered our prayers?" they questioned. "Doesn't He care about us?"

In the distance they could see the rain falling harder now, sending small rivulets running across the pathways. Hoping to inspire themselves with faith and confidence, the congregation began to sing. By now the sky was black overhead, and the rain pounded noisily on the church roof nearby. The rainy season had finally arrived in earnest. Wasn't God going to protect them? As other church members gathered from the surrounding villages, and arrived at the meeting place, they were amazed to discover that no rain was falling at their meeting place. The heavy drops were soaking the countryside all around, but their cleared worship area remained dry.

"How can this be?" the people asked.

Slowly the realization dawned on them that it wasn't raining where they were, although it was raining all around them.

"It's a miracle!" exclaimed the excited pastor. "God is keeping our meeting place dry. This is a real miracle!"

Excitement rippled through the congregation, for they knew God was answering their prayers. It was as though God had put up His big umbrella, and the church members were sheltered beneath it. With reverent awe the service continued.

The rains persisted week after week, sending the new shoots of maize sprouting out of the soaked ground. Yet every Sabbath the church members met in the dry, open clearing, free from the rain, amazed at the miracle God was performing on their behalf. With renewed faith, they sang with joy, making the wet hillsides resound with their exuberance.

Weeks later, as the pastor walked up the path toward the clearing, he did not hear the sound of singing coming from the clearing. Instead it was coming from the church building. Could it be? Could it really be?

When he reached the front door, he was amazed to discover that the chain and padlock were gone, and the people were inside! Triumpantly he entered the church building. Broad smiles from the church members greeted him. They were clearly happy to be back in their own church building again! Songs of thankful praise reverberated through the sanctuary.

That Sabbath it rained as usual—*and the meeting area where the church members had been holding their services under God's umbrella was soaking wet!* Now that they didn't need it any longer, God's umbrella was gone! But the memory of His miracle would stay with them as long as they lived—a reminder that God lives, that He cares for His earthly children, and that He is greater than man or the elements of nature.

Chapter 7
In Time of War

A war was being fought. Terrorists roamed the
countryside, looking for people to harass. Tension
filled the air. Especially worried were the many
church pastors whose churches and members were
scattered in various places throughout their districts.

"Oh, I wish you wouldn't go to the churches this
Sabbath," Pastor Muchema's wife pleaded one Friday
morning. "There is so much violence going on. Surely
our members will understand if you don't visit them
this once," she pleaded.

But Pastor Muchema would not be deterred. "I
must go," he told her. "The members need encourage-
ment now, more than ever." Then he added, "I know
that prayers are being offered on my behalf at the
union office this very morning, and I am confident
that God will care for me."

Together the pastor and his wife knelt in prayer,
pleading with God to protect him as he visited the
church members.

As the pastor started out on his bicycle, his wife
called out, "God go with you." Then added, "And with
your old, rickety bicycle."

Later she prayed again for divine protection for her

husband; then she busied herself with her housework in preparation for the Sabbath.

Pastor Muchema made a number of visits that Friday, encouraging those he met. By late afternoon he had arrived safely at a church member's home, where he stayed for the night.

Sabbath morning dawned crisp and clear, a perfect day for gathering some of the believers together for a worship service—a secret service, since at the time all worship was forbidden by the terrorists. Again Pastor Muchema started out on his bicycle, leaving behind a group of huts. He rode down a lonely path through bush country. Carefully he made his way over rocks and around thorn bushes.

He hadn't gone far when he heard a familiar hissing sound. Without looking he knew he had punctured a tire. He looked down, and, sure enough, one of the tires was flat. He stopped and pulled out his repair kit. He felt nervous as he worked, listening for any hint of approaching footsteps. He heard nothing. "It looks like I have nothing to fear," he sighed in relief. "But I must hurry!" Confidence mingled with tension seemed to slow his fingers as he groped for the repair kit in his case. Minutes ticked by as he worked. "Nearly finished now," he muttered to himself. But as he tightened one last nut, he heard voices and boots scuffing around just over a nearby rise.

He heard more footfalls. They were coming his way! There was no place to hide, no place to run. The scrub brush was sparsely scattered. There were no huts or roads in the area. The men's voices grew louder as they came closer.

"Oh God, protect me," he prayed.

Suddenly the men appeared—thirty of them— young men, tough-looking, intent on making trouble.

"What are you doing here?" demanded one tough-looking fellow, obviously their leader. "And who are you?"

Pastor Muchema told them he was a pastor just visiting some of his church members.

When they heard his explanation, they charged him with being a traitor. "You're a sellout, a traitor," they accused. "We don't need anyone like you around. Come with us."

The men pushed Pastor Muchema roughly ahead of them. Fear gripped his heart, for he knew he was in the midst of a gang of terrorists who were not in the habit of showing mercy.

Coming to a thicket, the terrorists began to threaten and insult the pastor. They searched everything he had. When they found a notebook, in which he had written the names of his church members, they demanded an explanation. He patiently told them what the names represented, but the men would not listen. He was glad that at least he had not brought with him the receipt book in which he kept his financial records. "If they found that on me," he thought, "they would shoot me immediately."

"We know your kind," the terrorists charged. "You take money from fathers and mothers and give it to the white man." With that the terrorists began beating up Pastor Muchema. They hit him time and again.

Thrusting his songbook into his hands, the evil men sneered, "Sing! Sing one of your songs to us."

The pastor began to sing in a faltering voice. Almost at once one of the men silenced him by beating him over the head with a stick. Dazed and bleeding, he watched helplessly as they tore his Bible to pieces. Then they grabbed his songbook and destroyed it. Next his empty briefcase was ripped apart.

"Now that should silence your nonsense!" they

shouted, their guns swinging menacingly by their sides.

Although his fate appeared sealed, the terrorists seemed uncertain as to what to do next. So, they forced him back against a tree and secured him with heavy ropes.

"We're going to go and decide what to do with you," said their leader. "We will tie you to this tree, so you can't get away." The leader laughed a cynical, wicked laugh. "And," he continued, "if you try to get away, I will shoot you immediately."

"Oh, God," pleaded Pastor Muchema silently, "take away their hatred as they meet together and reach a decision about what to do with me. Please spare my life, if it is Your will. If I must die, comfort my wife and family." A strange peace came over the pastor as he prayed.

Some thirty minutes passed, although it seemed much longer, as Pastor Muchema stood, tied to the tree, wondering what the fateful decision of the terrorists would be. Finally three men returned.

Without explanation they gruffly untied him and commanded, "Follow us."

They marched off into the bush, following no trail in particular. The sun beat down mercilessly. After a while the men found some shade and sprawled out on the ground. With nothing else to do, they began questioning their captive. "Who is this Jesus your Bible talks so much about?" one asked.

Uncertain of the purpose of their question, Pastor Muchema answered simply, "I believe Jesus is the Son of God."

As if jabbed with a fiery needle, one of the young men leaped to his feet shouting, "That is enough evidence! Let's kill him here and now. That will silence him forever."

Calmly the pastor responded, "You can kill me, but God's words will live forever. I am not afraid to die."

"Kill him!" shouted the angry young man.

Expressing their uncertainty, the other two men got up slowly, annoyance written on their faces. Abruptly they commanded, "Come on, let's get moving."

Grumbling his discontent, the third man followed, obviously unhappy with the situation.

By evening the men reached a village. Here they requisitioned blankets of the villagers and bedded themselves down a little distance from Pastor Muchema.

Late that night the men were awakened by loud talking. It was the other twenty-seven terrorists who had been with them earlier that day.

"You man of God," they barked at the pastor, "are you still alive?" They seemed surprised to discover he had not been shot.

As they bedded down for the night, one young man spread his blanket down nearer the pastor than the others and quietly began to question him about his faith. Pastor Muchema sensed that, beneath his tough exterior, this man was sincerely seeking for something better.

Long into the night they talked, until the young fellow abruptly ended the conversation with a curt, "Tomorrow you will be shot."

Pastor Muchema reviewed his life carefully, making sure everything was right with his God. Finally he fell asleep, prepared to die, yet confident that God was able to deliver him, if that was in His plan.

Early the next morning, long before the sunrise, the terrorists woke Pastor Muchema. "This is your final day," they jeered. "Get up! We're going to shoot you."

The tough-looking gang stood around their commander. "Let's finish him off," urged the young terrorist who had demanded his execution the previous day; his impatience seemed to permeate the group.

The commander turned his back to the group and bent his head downward as he deliberated. Pastor Muchema prayed earnestly. He knew his fate was being decided. Again a feeling of calm flooded his soul. He was prepared for whatever was decided.

As the seconds ticked by, the angry terrorist who the day before had called for the pastor's death, kicked impatiently at a stone. "Come on, come on. Let's get it over with," he urged.

At last the commander looked up. Just then an old man walked by. "Old man," demanded the terrorist leader. "Do you know this man?" He pointed to the pastor.

The old man stopped. Pastor Muchema did not recognize him. What would he say? He sensed that his fate hinged on the old man's answer. The old man paused a moment; then in a clear voice he responded, "Yes, I know him. He is a Seventh-day Adventist pastor."

"Is he a sellout?" asked the commander.

"No," answered the old man without hesitation.

Turning to Pastor Muchema, the commander said, "We respect you. Go back to your Bible and pray to your Jesus and your God. You are free." A look of kindness softened the terrorist's hardened features.

The impatient terrorist leapt forward, "But . . . but he . . ."

The commander interrupted, "I'm in charge here!" Then to the pastor, "Don't say a word about what has happened to anyone, or you will not get off so easy next time."

Pastor Muchema turned and walked out of the circle of tough-looking desperadoes. When he turned to thank the old man, he was nowhere in sight. "Was he an angel of God?" wondered the pastor.

Pastor Muchema rejoiced as he walked back to his home through one village after another. News of his providential deliverance had preceded him.

"How did you escape?" the people asked in amazement. "How did you get away? We were sure you were dead by now."

Pastor Muchema responded with great confidence, "The same God who delivered Daniel from the lions' den is still delivering His people today. God hasn't changed; He is just the same today."

Today Pastor Muchema and his family continue to minister to the spiritual needs of the people in their district. They witness to the greatness of God, encouraging and strengthening the believers wherever they go.

Chapter 8
And the Message Goes On

Far up in the hills of Malawi lie the Kirk Mountains that separate the uncertain activities of Mozambique from the quiet, serene life of Malawi.

Many small churches dot the hillsides. Some of them are constructed of red brick and mud; others are whitewashed and gleam in the golden sun. Few of these churches know Bible truths as taught by the Seventh-day Adventists. The Catholics, Methodists, and other churches established missions in these hills long before Adventists made their way into this area. So when the Adventists began work here, they discovered that their message went slowly and encountered fierce opposition. Men of determination, men filled with God's Spirit, were the only ones who did not give in to discouragement.

Pastor Mkhala was made of this kind of mettle. Appointed pastor of one of the districts, he prayed each day for divine guidance in his work. Filled with enthusiasm, he began Bible study groups. Small when they began, these groups at first attracted little attention. But as more people began attending and their numbers increased, the local preachers of the established established church became concerned.

"We can't allow these Adventist come in here and

corrupt our members," complained one disturbed preacher. "Something has to be done."

"My church used to be so peaceful, but lately some of my members are coming to me and asking questions about things that shouldn't make any difference to them. They come with Bibles under their arms and want me to give them answers. Many times I don't know what to tell them. They are getting all confused by those 'Seven-day' people. I think we should get rid of them, get them out of our peaceful Kirk Mountains."

And so this irate preacher soon met with the local chief, who listened with a sympathetic ear to this preacher's complaint.

"Yes, yes," agreed the young chief, anxious to please everyone. "We can't have this confusion in our peaceful mountains. I gave this pastor my permission to establish churches, but I did not know what a stir he would cause. I will not allow this 'Seven-day' teacher to spread unrest in my area. I want him out! Now!" The chief's voice rose to a high pitch, so that any passerby could hear.

When Pastor Mkhala learned about the young chief's decision, he requested a meeting with the other chief of this village area. The latter was an old man, wise in years and well respected by those in his territory. As Pastor Mkhala asked about permission to hold Bible studies in the area, the old chief nodded agreement.

"It is good to know what the Bible says," he declared. "My people need to learn and follow its words." So the Bible studies continued, with the wizened old chief's family occasionally listening in on them.

It wasn't long before the preacher of the established church learned that Pastor Mkhala was not leaving. "In fact, he has permission to stay and continue his Bible studies," reported one little old woman.

"Who gave him permission?" demanded the prejudiced preacher, his face contorted with anger. "I was assured he would be expelled from our village. Who told him he could stay?"

"The old chief," answered one of the village women with a look of triumph.

"Humph!" snorted the preacher. "Just wait until he hears from *me*. He'll change his mind. The Bible-toting teacher will be out of here in no time!"

But all the pleading and cajoling did not change the old chief 's mind. He had made a decision—a wise decision, he thought—and he refused to be moved.

A bit deflated, the preacher mulled over in his mind how he could stop the 'Seven-day' teacher. Scheme after scheme was devised in his dark head, until he settled on one idea he was sure would chase the Adventist preacher out of those hills.

Gathering a group of noisy youngsters, he convinced them that the best place to play a rousing game of soccer was right next to the Bible study meetinghouse. And the best time to play was when the thatched house was filled with people. The louder the yells, the better the game, he assured them. The boys, eager to play their game, willingly complied.

Day after day, whenever people gathered to hear Pastor Mkhala teach God's Word, a gang of rowdies simultaneously appeared with a soccer ball. Shouts and yells pierced the air. Unable to shut out the noise because the meeting place had no windows or doors, the people inside the meeting house had to strain to hear the pastor's words.

Pastor Mkhala prayed that God would intervene to stop the disturbances. He feared that the people would become tired of hearing him, as well as the competition, and would stop attending. "Please do something, Lord," he pleaded.

His prayers seemed to go unanswered. Every time the soccer players returned, their whooping and hollering continued undiminished. But Pastor Mkhala noticed something that surprised him. In spite of the competition, the people faithfully returned to the meetings. Day after day they crowded into the meetinghouse to hear God's Word presented in a way they had never heard before. So intent were they upon listening to the pastor's messages, they barely noticed the noise outside.

This went on for three weeks. At the end of this time, when Pastor Mkhala made an appeal for those who wanted to become members of the Seventh-day Adventist Church, eleven people came forward—living witnesses that God's truth is greater than all the noise, shouts, and taunts of the opposition.

After the baptism, the Bible studies continued, and the message of God's love began to spread throughout the region. Thus it is with God's message. It will go on in spite of opposition. God lives and His truth will triumph gloriously!

Chapter 9
Bus-Stop Evangelism

Mrs. Masala looked at her watch. Yes, she was right on time. "The bus should arrive any minute now," she said to herself as she sat on her upturned suitcase. "I do hope it won't be late!" She sighed as she thought of the important lectures she planned to attend in Arusha and how frequently the buses were behind schedule.

As she waited, her mind drifted to the sounds coming from a large tent nearby. The sound of singing wafted across the air—songs she knew well from her own church. Absentmindedly she hummed along. "Must be another religious meeting," she mused. "Seems like there's preaching everywhere these days. Ah, that's the way it should be. Religion will do this world good."

Her thoughts went back to her various duties in the Catholic church, of which she was a member. She hoped she had not forgotten any arrangements, so that others would have to carry out her assignments during her month's absence.

Tomorrow her husband would be attending Sunday mass without her. She sighed, "Yes, following a religion is what this world needs." She looked at her watch. "Where is that bus?" she muttered.

While she was thinking, the singing stopped, and now she could hear a man's voice coming through the open tent. Mrs. Masala listened to his words. The preacher was talking about Jesus' birth. How often she had heard this story—it was as well known to her as to the preacher.

Suddenly all her attention focused on the meaning of his words. This was more than just the same old story of Jesus. The preacher kept saying something about love and forgiveness. It seemed so personal. It sounded like a new story meant just for her.

The minutes flew by. The bus didn't arrive. Mrs. Masala continued to listen, a desire and hope taking hold of her in a way she had never before experienced. She wanted to know more about *this* Jesus.

The preacher spoke of Jesus as though He were our personal friend, as though He were Someone who cared about *her* troubles, about *her* problems. Mrs. Masala was captivated by the words of the speaker. She completely forgot about her bus. Eagerly she listened to the preacher's words. When he invited the congregation to give their lives to the Lord, Mrs. Masala responded gladly. She got up from her seat on her suitcase and walked into the tent, up the aisle, and stood directly in front of the pulpit, her suitcase in her hand. Tears of joy streamed down her cheeks.

After the meeting, the preacher greeted her warmly. His friendliness made her feel at ease immediately. When he introduced himself as a Seventh-day Adventist pastor, her previous hesitancy about these people vanished in her determination to learn more.

Just then she heard the horn of her long-awaited bus. Bidding the preacher goodbye, she hastened to the bus, a new understanding lightening her steps.

Weeks later her convictions continued as strong as ever. She sought to learn more. When she returned home, she eagerly looked up the local Seventh-day Adventist church. She was received warmly and joined the baptismal class, drinking in all the new-found truths she heard.

However, before long her parents heard about their daughter's "strange" ideas. They immediately sent the local Catholic priest to counsel her to return to her family's church. The priest was unsuccessful in his endeavor. So her parents came to her home to try to persuade her not to become a Seventh-day Adventist.

When they stated their objections, Mrs. Masala calmly took her Bible and began to answer their questions with verses she had recently learned. As she read and effectively answered her parents' objections, their faces became distorted with anger. In their fury they began to beat her. "We'll make you change your mind," they screamed.

As the blows fell upon her, Mrs. Masala began to sing songs she had learned at the Adventist church. Cursing and swearing, her parents became more infuriated. "You'll never be part of our family again," they cried in anger. "We disown you! You are not our daughter any longer!—not until you give up these strange and foolish ideas!" Then they stomped out of her house. Their curses continued to explode until they were too far away to be heard anymore. Mrs. Masala fell to her knees sobbing.

Not many weeks after this, Mrs. Masala and her husband were baptized together in a stream near the Seventh-day Adventist church. They rejoiced in their new-found faith and wanted to share it with others, in spite of their family's hostility.

Filled with enthusiasm, they began work as literature evangelists. They moved to the Uganda border and worked in the Bukoba area, where many Roman Catholics live. The Lord richly blessed their efforts, and in a short time a group of people were faithfully meeting every Sabbath under the trees.

Today, after taking a ministerial course, Mr. Masala is pastoring a group of churches. And Mrs. Masala? She continues to sell Christian literature, her enthusiasm for Christ shedding hope and love to everyone she meets. She is a living testimony that God lives—and that His power is greater than all obstacles. It is a power that changes lives!

Chapter 10
God Never Forgot

Elizabeth was born into a Seventh-day Adventist Christian home. Her mother wanted her to grow up to serve her God, so she taught her to obey God and sent her to the best schools she could find.

When Elizabeth finished secondary school, she went to a large city where she trained to become a nurse. Upon completion of her training, she began work in a large hospital in the city. While there, she met a young man, Mr. Katenga, who was a member of another denomination. They became friends, and their friendship eventually led to marriage—contrary to her mother's wishes and what her mother had taught her.

Before long Elizabeth and her husband went to the country of Zambia to work. Elizabeth again found work in a hospital. She began attending her husband's church with him. Eventually she cast aside her Seventh-day Adventist upbringing.

When Malawi gained its independence, Mr. Katenga, who had been born in that country, decided to return to his homeland. Before long both he and his wife began to take an active part in the social and civic affairs of his country. In time, when the Malawi government began looking for an ambassador to the United States, it chose Mr. Katenga.

So Elizabeth, with her husband and children, sailed

to the United States to represent their country in Washington. While they were in America, Mr. Katenga felt that his children should receive their education in a Christian school. He scouted around and chose a Seventh-day Adventist school in the area. While Elizabeth was happy that her children could attend a Christian school, she felt no desire to return to the church of her childhood. On the contrary, she continued to attend her husband's church with him.

After several years the Katengas were transferred to the United Kingdom. Later he served as ambassador for his country in several other countries, including West Germany and Ethiopia.

After a number of years Mr. Katenga returned with his family to Malawi and settled in the city of Blantyre. About a year later, tragedy struck. Mr. Katenga died suddenly. Elizabeth, with her three daughters and two sons, were left to face the future without a father and husband. Grief-stricken, Elizabeth struggled through each day, continuing her work with the Malawi Railways Nursing Association. Friends from around the world expressed their sympathies, but the sorrow because of her loss was always very near.

Although she continued to attend her husband's church, God seemed far away. She was sure He had forgotten her. Then one Saturday morning, as she was doing some shopping, she heard a voice speak to her. She heard it distinctly. It said, "Return your tithe to the Lord." She was surprised. Who had spoken? She turned around, but saw no one.

"Return my tithe?" she questioned. "I haven't paid tithe since I left the Seventh-day Adventist Church years ago. Why should I pay tithe now?" She had a good-paying job, and even though her husband was dead, she didn't lack money. But pay tithe? Why be bothered? She knew that the Seventh-day Adventist church taught its members to pay tithe, but that was the least thing she had on her mind. She determined to ignore the strange voice.

Two days went by, and she didn't think much about the voice. And then as she was on her way to work, she heard clearly the same words, "Return your tithe to the Lord."

"Can't I get away from this voice?" she spoke out loud with disgust. "I don't want anything to do with the Adventist Church."

But as time went on, the words of that unseen messenger haunted Elizabeth. Everywhere she turned, it seemed, she was reminded that she should pay her tithe. She couldn't escape that voice.

About eleven o'clock one Sabbath morning, Elizabeth quietly slipped into a back seat of a little Adventist church in Blantyre. As the offering was collected, she placed an envelope in the offering plate, and as soon as church was over, she left. No one noticed she had been in attendance.

Although the church members did not notice her presence that morning, those who counted the tithes and offerings did notice her generous contribution and that the envelope was marked "tithe."

Elizabeth continued faithfully to come incognito to the little Adventist church for many months, at first for the sole purpose of paying her tithe and salving her conscience. But little by little a feeling of peace began to seep into her life.

One Sabbath morning, as she prepared to go to the church to turn in her tithe, she felt impressed to attend another, smaller Adventist church. She didn't know why. It was farther away than the church she had been attending, and she had never been there before, but she went anyway.

When she got to the church, she found a large group

of children outside and asked them whether or not there was going to be a service.

"Oh yes," the children eagerly responded. "The service is going to be held down in the pine grove. It is camp-meeting time, and that is where the meeting is going to be today."

Elizabeth made her way down the hill to the pine grove, where the people were gathered. Quietly she took her place among them and listened to the words of the preacher. As she listened, every word seemed to be spoken directly to her. Never before had she been so moved by a sermon.

When at the close the preacher made an appeal for those who had been backsliders to renew their commitment to the Lord Jesus before it was too late, Elizabeth Katenga was one of the first to stand. Moved, it seemed, by an unseen hand, she took her place with the others who responded, in front of the pulpit. She was filled with awe that the Lord had led her here to this gathering on this particular Sabbath.

At the close of the service, when the pastors asked for the names and addresses of those who had come forward, Elizabeth gave them hers. Two weeks later Pastor Armer called at her well-furnished home and was invited in.

After the customary formal introduction and a few minutes of casual talking, the pastor politely ventured, "Mrs. Katenga, tell us about yourself."

Slowly at first, Elizabeth told the pastor the story of her life, how in spite of the fact that she had turned away from her mother's teachings, God had not given up on her. Then she added hastily, "I want to make it clear that I do not want to become a Seventh-day Adventist again. I am satisfied with the church of my late husband. At the same time, I believe I should return my tithe to the church, and I will continue to give it to the Seventh-day Adventist Church. I intend to do this because God has spoken to me, and my husband's church does not practice tithe paying."

Pastor Armer did not allow Elizabeth's statement to discourage him. He believed that God was leading this woman to the church through the avenue of tithing, even though she did not seem prepared to rejoin the church of her childhood just then. Without reacting to her statement, he diplomatically offered to study the Bible with her. She agreed.

In this way the pastor began fifteen months of weekly Bible studies in Elizabeth's home. Every Friday evening Elizabeth and her son listened and shared in the study of the Bible. At the end of this time the two were baptized into the Seventh-day Adventist church by the pastor of the little Kabula Hill Church. How grateful she was that, although she had given up on God, He had not given up on her. At the right moment, and with just the words she needed, the Holy Spirit had led her back to God's remnant church, and she resolved to follow her Master faithfully once again.

Today, Elizabeth Katenga is taking an active part in the leadership of the Seventh-day Adventist Church where she lives. She knows that God's love is greater than any human love. She knows, because God never forgot her through all the years she was wandering away from Him. How wonderful that the God we serve lives and never lets us go.

Chapter 11
Bandits!

The chilly wind ripped around the corners of the stone school buildings, howling its eerie way into the moonless woods. Munemo tossed restlessly on his bed. "Would sleep never come?" he wondered. Standing in as headmaster for a school of 400 students was no easy job, especially because of all the political unrest that had his country in turmoil, with its stories of bandits marauding the countryside.

Munemo turned toward the wall, hoping to find comfort and sleep. His body relaxed, but his mind continued to whirl. He tried to push aside his uneasy thoughts. "I guess it must just be the restless wind," he fretted. "We've prayed with all the students for God's protection. I must trust Him to care for us. God has kept us safe these past six months since the overseas workers were evacuated, surely He'll continue His care . . . ." Before he realized it, he had drifted off into a troubled sleep.

Meanwhile, not far away, a group of dark-skinned men huddled around a fire, gleaming swords within easy reach. One man, bigger than the others, with broad shoulders and muscles bulging from under his khaki shirt, spoke, his voice low and sinister, "I tell you men, it's time we take that 'Seven-day' school! We've delayed too long already. It should have been ours long ago."

The big man stood on a raised platform, as though trying to emphasize what he was about to say by his height.

Towering high above the fire, wind-tossed flames casting eerie shadows across his dark face, making it appear frightening even to his men. The leader spat out his words. "Tonight is the night we kill! Tonight it will be Munemo! We've discussed it before, but tonight! *Tonight* is the night!" He repeated *tonight* for emphasis.

Then, raising his sword with a muscular grip, he grabbed the hair of the man nearest him. "This is the way we will kill Munemo!" he said, yanking up the seated man by the hair of his head and flashing his sword across his neck. The man jerked away, just in time, leaving a fistful of black, curly hair in the leader's hand.

The bandits seated around the big man grunted their approval, a glint of evil hiding any fear that might have been reflected in their eyes.

Animated discussion followed, focusing on how to "get" Munemo once they broke through the woods surrounding the school buildings.

One of the seated men had a suggestion. "Once we take possession of the school, we'll need cattle to graze the land to give us wealth for bartering."

The others nodded agreement. "Go on, go on," they urged, eagerly listening to the man's plan.

"I suggest we get the cows while we're on the way. By so doing, we'll be ready to set ourselves up in business when we arrive at the school. We need cattle, plenty of cattle! We need a herd like they have over at Dube's Ranch. We should go by that ranch first, take the cows, then go on to the school. That would save a trip back to get the cows."

An argument arose. The leader wanted it understood that the school property was his and that the bandits were going to the school first. But after further arguments, the bandits agreed to steal the Dube Ranch cows first. Smothering their campfire, they threw on their jackets and moved off into the night. This wasn't their first "job." These men were hardened criminals. They had numerous thefts and murders to their credit. Cattle stealing was easy work for them, and it wasn't long until Dube's Ranch had been stripped of its cattle.

After the gang drove their newly commandeered cattle into a holding pen, they stopped for a drink at a small tavern along the way to the school. As they gloated over their success, they downed one beer after the other.

"Bring out the homemade stuff," they demanded raucously. "We want real booze with which to celebrate. Tonight's a big night for us. We're taking over the 'Seven-day' school!"

About this time another group of bandits appeared at the tavern. Their leader, a fiery little fellow, had a temper to match. He had once been a member of the big man's gang, but a disagreement had arisen, and they had separated. Since that time, they had stayed clear of each other.

What brought them together this cold, windy night nobody seems to know. Perhaps it was the chill wind pushing them toward the same small tavern for a bit of warmth and a drink of liquor to settle their edgy nerves.

The big man boasted loudly, as he invited the other gang members to join him, "Come celebrate our victory! Before morning the 'Seven-day' school will be ours!" The leader's contemptuous laugh echoed off the battered, thin walls of the tavern. "Wouldn't you like to join us in our kill? The 'Seven-day' school is an easy target! Come along," he urged.

The Adventist school lay asleep in the stillness of the night. The wind had died down to a low rustle in the trees as the night wore on. Mrs. Munemo rose to tend their crying baby; then she returned to bed beside her snoring husband. In the girls' dorm Martha, one of the girl students, awakened by a hacking cough, stumbled sleepily to the sink for a drink of water. About the same time Robert, one of the male students, opened his sleep-laden eyes to see his roommate bent over his history book, the shadows thrown by his candle flickering across its pages. Robert peered at his watch—2:30 a.m.

"That guy is really devoted to his schoolwork," he mused. In less than a minute Robert was sound asleep again.

3:00 a.m.: The night watchman completed his rounds and sat down with his feet against the tool shed. His eyelids drooping heavily.

4:00 a.m.: Munemo turned in bed. A rooster crows.

5:00 a.m.: Light begins breaking through the dark night clouds. The night watchman rises groggily and begins his rounds.

5:15 a.m.: A jacket-clad man comes running from the woods. His heavy footfalls beating rhythmically as he crosses the clearing, heading straight for the Munemos' house. He bounds up the two wooden steps, the pounding of his boots jarring the early morning stillness. Munemos' baby cries. The night watchman looks over from the boys' dorm just in time to see the runner raise his arm. His loud rapping on the door echoes across campus. Silence.

The runner paces back and forth, his chest heaving with exhaustion, his face etched with tension.

The door creaks open, and Munemo stands inside, blinking sleep from his eyes.

In his haste the African omits the customary greetings and blurts out breathlessly, "Mr. Munemo! What a relief to see you alive this morning! Did you know you were supposed to be killed last night by the bandits?"

Munemo shakes his head in disbelief; his eyes are large and fully awake now. Mrs. Munemo comes up behind him, baby in arms, as the runner rambles on with his story.

"The bandits were going to take over the school last night. They were going to kill you, but something strange happened. I've just this minute come from the small tavern down in the village." The man paused to catch his breath. "There was a fight there early this morning. Two gangs got into an argument. They drew their swords and. . . . " His words tumbled over each other in his excitement.

"It seems that the small man's gang was bent on settling a score by getting rid of the leader of the other gang, and before anyone knew what was happening, the big leader lay on the floor dead, his head chopped off. I saw it myself!"

The messenger paused. After a moment's silence, he quietly continued, "That big leader had vowed he was going to kill you. Instead, he is lying on the tavern floor, dead. You're a lucky man, Mr. Munemo."

Having finished his story, the runner slowly backed down the steps, one step at a time, his eyes not moving from Munemo. "You're a lucky man. Lucky! Lucky indeed!" he repeated. He stared at Munemo and his wife standing in the open doorway, as though not sure whether to believe his own eyes. Then, without another word, he turned and ran back through the woods the way he had come.

Later that morning the sounds of music burst forth from the school's assembly hall. The melodious strains wafted over the early morning air, permeating the cold woods with their echoes of praise. In Africa, when 400 students join together to thank God for protecting their leader and their school, the surrounding villages hear about it!

What a praise meeting the students had that morning! There was no doubt in their minds that God had intervened to thwart the evil plans of the enemies of their school. There was no doubt in their minds that God lives and that He is great—greater than the toughest gangs, greater than their evil schemes.

(Munemo, a mere teacher, continued to be in charge of that school for over nine months, until peace was restored to the area. The principal then returned, giving Munemo a much-needed rest.)

Chapter 12
Fire! Fire!

Okelo woke groggily. What had he heard that awoke him? He peered through the thatching of the wall of his hut. It was still pitch-dark outside, not time to get up yet and do the plowing.

Something had awakened him. But what? He listened. All was quiet, except for the faint mooing of a cow in a nearby pasture. Then he smelled it. Smoke! Okelo sniffed again to make sure. Suddenly he was wide awake, every muscle tensed. This was no ordinary cooking fire! The smoke was too strong; too close. Suddenly it dawned on Okelo what had happened.

Because of the long, hot summer days, the thatching on the roofs of African huts tended to become bone dry and ripe for spontaneous combustion or the slightest spark. Such happenings were all too common. Okelo had seen this happen many times.

Sometimes a spark would land unnoticed in the dry thatching, carried on the breeze from a woman's cooking fire. There the spark would smolder, unnoticed, sometimes for hours. Then, suddenly, it would burst into flames. In a matter of minutes all that would be left would be ashes where once had stood an African hut.

"Wake up! Wake up! Our house is on fire!" shouted Okelo. Instantly his wife and four children sprang up from their mats. "Run! Run! Our house is burning!" yelled Okelo, grabbing up his youngest boy and ducking out the door and into the cool night air. His wife and the three older children quickly followed. By now the roof of his hut was engulfed in flames, lighting up the entire village.

Five-year-old Ben tugged at his mother's skirt. "My slingshot! I want my slingshot!" he wailed. "Uncle just finished making it for me. Please let me go back in and get it. It's right at the head of my sleeping mat. Please."

Mother grabbed Ben's arm tightly, "No one is going back in that burning house," she said. "You would never get back out alive!"

Okelo, overhearing his son's plea, suddenly remembered the family Bible, "The Bible! Our precious family Bible!" he cried out in panic. "I must get it!"

Okelo looked around and ckecked to see that all his family had gotten out safely from the burning house. It was then that he realized he had been so concerned about the safety of his wife and children that he had not thought about the Bible until now.

"Oh, why did I forget!" Okelo chided himself. He turned toward the burning hut. Smoke was billowing out of its crooked wooden door.

"I'm going to get it." He spoke with quiet determination. "I must get it. I know where it is. It's on the table, right where I left it last night."

"No," shouted his wife, clutching at his arm. "You mustn't go back inside!"

"But I have to get the Bible! It's our most precious possession!" With that Okelo wrenched himself free from his wife's hold.

"No!" she screamed. "Come back!" But it was too late.

By now other villagers had arrived to watch help-lessly as Okelo's house burned to the ground.

"Come back!" they shouted, echoing Okelo's wife's words. "You'll never make it back. Don't be a fool! Don't go!" they warned.

Okelo pushed open the wooden door, and dashed in-side briefly, but the flames were too much for him and he staggered back. The entire hut was a raging inferno. Bitter disappointment was etched across his dark face as he retreated to his wife's side. He spoke no words—his grief was too keen. Their precious fami-ly Bible was gone!

Little Sarah looked up into her father's face. "Father," she said with childlike faith, "God can save our Bible. I know He can. We must ask Him."

Okelo wasn't so sure, yet he obligingly bowed his head as Sarah folded her hands and prayed. After all, he felt he could not betray her childlike faith. But realistically he knew nothing could survive in a fire as hot as this.

After the fire had died down and only embers remained, the family trudged with heavy hearts to Grandma's hut, where they stayed the remainder of the night.

Long after the village was quiet and the family had fallen into a fitful sleep, Okelo lay awake thinking. "Why, oh why, didn't I immediately think of the Bible?" he reproached himself. "I could easily have grabbed it up, and it would have been safe. Why, oh why, couldn't I have thought of it? Why didn't God remind me? Didn't He care?"

Okelo had had to save money for many months before he had enough to buy that Bible. How hard he had worked, planting and hoeing, harvesting and sell-ing. And then, when he had enough money, he had gone to the Kamagambo Adventist College store and had purchased the large family Bible with the smooth black cover. Now it was gone. "Why did God let it happen?" he grieved. And yet, there were things Okelo could be thankful for. No one had gotten injured.

Slowly little Sarah's faith penetrated through to Okelo's consciousness. "Maybe . . . maybe God *did* save their Bible," he thought. "Maybe God did answer Sarah's simple prayer." Sarah had prayed with such confidence.

This glimmer of hope was snuffed out as the night breeze brought the fresh scent of smoke to Okelo's nostrils. Dark reality engulfed him once again. His house and all he had owned was now only a pile of ashes, and he had failed to rescue the Bible. He turned his face to the wall, wishing he could pray, wishing he could hope.

As soon as daylight came, the village began to stir, as the normal routine of activity began in the African village. But for Okelo and his family, this would be not be a normal day. They had lost everything.

They had to face the cold fact that they had no house, no clothes, no pots of mealies, no table, and worst of all, no Bible. No Bible for Father Okelo to read aloud from each morning and evening, while his family listened in solemn reverence. No leather-covered Bible for Okelo to proudly touch each time he passed it as it lay in its special place on the table. It was gone!

Later that morning, some of the villagers came to Okelo and offered to help him build a new hut. "We're ready to help you. We'll begin today!" they promised. "Where do you want to build? On the same plot or somewhere else?"

Many of the villagers—men and women, boys and girls—followed Okelo and his family as they sadly walked back to the place where their hut had stood. The ashes were cold now. The early morning dew clustered like sorrowing tears on the blackened remains. Okelo kicked dejectedly at the ashes. A cloud of gray particles rose around him.

Suddenly, he kicked something solid. It caught his attention. He stopped, stooped down, and looked. What could it be? Feeling with his fingers, he grasped the hard object. He couldn't believe his eyes. It was his precious Bible! A small cry of joy escaped his lips.

An instant later little Sarah was at his side. "What is it, Father? What have you found?"

Okelo lifted the object. "The Bible!" Sarah squealed. "Our family Bible. God really did save it! I knew He could!" She danced merrily around, sending ashes flying everywhere.

Okelo stood to his full height and gazed at the Bible clutched in his trembling hands. Reverently he blew away the last ashes that covered it. Its pages were unsinged, its cover unscratched!

Okelo's heart nearly burst with joy. "Oh, thank You, God," he exclaimed. "I will always love You."

The villagers that had accompanied him looked on in amazement, too awed to speak a word. A solemn reverence filled the place. God seemed very near.

For days and weeks the story of how the God of heaven lives and is greater than fire, and how in answer to a little girl's prayer He had saved the holy Bible from burning up was told and retold from one village to another.

"Surely this God is a great God," they said in awe.

As a result of this miracle many people praised God's name and believed on Him.

Chapter 13
The Miracle Church

The little church rang with sounds of glorious music, every member singing in perfect harmony, their voices blending together with contented enthusiasm. They had every reason to sing! For they had their own church building in which to meet each Sabbath. This was a church they had sacrificed to build. Yes, they had been blessed, and their singing resounded with praise.

Without warning the singers' contented enthusiasm was interrupted by loud pounding at the front door. Harsh voices cut through the harmony of the songs. The melodious singing came to a faltering halt, as the members, in unison, turned their heads to see what the commotion was all about.

A group of men, some clad in the uniforms of the government police, stomped into the church, their heavy hobnail boots pounding out their demand for attention.

Silently the church members watched as the ruthless men surveyed the church, measuring its size from wall to wall. Then their leader announced, "We will set up here! This is ideal for our local office." His raucous voice shattered the reverence of the sanctuary.

Turning to the silent, wide-eyed church members he announced, "This is not your church anymore. Our government offices will move in today. We want this building vacated immediately!"

The church members stared at each other in shocked disbelief. They had been worshiping peacefully just a minute before; now they were being ordered to leave their house of worship.

For a long moment they sat in stunned silence, as though glued to their pews, too benumbed to move.

"Well, don't just sit there! I said I want this building vacated immediately! Now get out!" yelled the officer.

As though in a dream the church members stood, then with hesitant steps walked out, loathe to leave their precious church where they had come each week to listen to the messages from God's Word.

Once outside, the members looked at each other in bewildered disbelief.

Taking the situation in hand, their optimistic leader suggested, "Let's go under the tree on the nearby hillside and continue our church service. We can still worship God even though we no longer have our church."

Waking to the realization that they had no other meeting place, the members gathered under the spreading branches of an acacia tree, where they continued their services. They wondered if they would ever worship in their church again. As they prayed, their prayers were filled with the request, "Please, God, make it possible for us to worship in our church again."

It wasn't long until the government officials brought in their desks and typewriters, chairs and tables, and set them up in the church. It was clear that they intended to stay for a long, long while.

But one day a swarm of bees flew in through an open window. More bees followed, until the room was buzzing with the insects. They landed on the desks, got inside the typewriters, and appeared to be taking over.

The government office workers ran out the door yelling, "Bees! Bees! Get them out of here!" But in spite of all the spraying and swatting, the bees remained.

"I'm not going back in there to work!" the workers declared. "We simply have to move out."

So the moving vans came and loaded up all the desks and typewriters, tables and chairs, and left the church to the bees.

Sabbath came. The church members looked inside their church. All was quiet. Gone was the government office equipment—*and the bees!*

"God has answered our prayers!" they rejoiced. They entered their church with gladness and held their services in their beloved church once more. They found not a bee in the place.

However, it wasn't long before word got back to the government officials that the bees had vacated the premises and the church members had resumed services in the place. Boldly the officials returned, stomping their boots as loudly as before. Again they arrogantly ordered the worshipers, "Out!"

The church members dutifully obeyed. This time, however, they didn't feel as dejected as the first time the order was given. After all, hadn't God worked a miracle for them once? If He did it once, surely He could do it again.

The desks and typewriters, tables and chairs returned to the little church. The officials sat down to carry on their business. Meanwhile the church members watched and prayed with eager anticipation.

Suddenly a cry came from inside the building. "Snakes! Snakes!"

Incredible as it may seem, snakes slithered across the floor. Snakes hung from the rafters. There were snakes everywhere! The workers rushed out of the building yelling, "Get those snakes out of there!" But the snakes had come to stay—at least temporarily.

Soon the government moving vans appeared again. The desks and typewriters, tables and chairs were loaded onto them and taken away.

The next Sabbath the excited church members returned to their church and held services. There wasn't a snake to be found anywhere. Tears of joy were mingled with songs of praise as they realized that this was truly a miracle of God.

Weeks went by, and no government officials returned. Months have now passed, and every week the church members meet in their "miracle church" to praise God for His great miracle-working power.